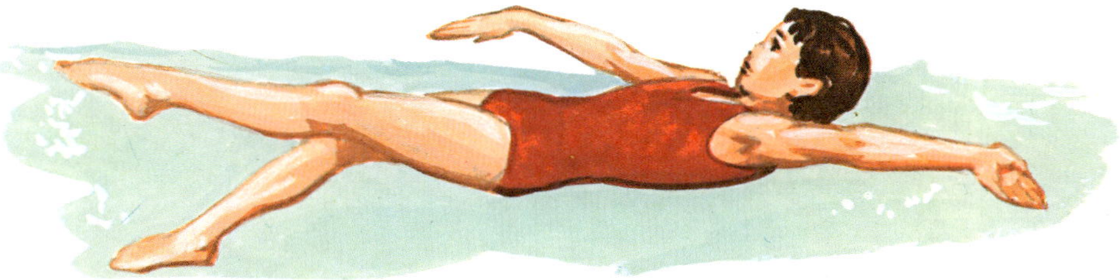

Can you name the strokes these swimmers are performing, and explain what their hands and feet are doing in each case? You can check your answers on pages 19, 23, 27 and 30.

LEARNING TO SWIM

by Hugh Hamilton Smith

Devised and created by Mercury Books
First published in 1973 by William Collins Sons and Co. Ltd., Glasgow and London

ISBN 0 00 103321 2
Printed in Tenerife (Spain) by Litografia A. Romero, S.A.

AND DIVE

all in colour

CONTENTS

COLLINS · GLASGOW AND LONDON

Champions start at the shallow end

Swimming is a sport that is full of different satisfactions. You can swim indoors or outdoors, as one of a group or alone. You can swim for fun, or for physical fitness, or for the challenge. You can swim to prove something or to win something, or you can – just swim. Young people swim; older people swim; people all over the world swim. For some of them it is a pleasant pastime to enjoy on a warm sunny day at a nearby beach; for others it is a highly competitive sport demanding long hours of training and gruelling effort all the year round.

Whether you become a once-a-year vacation dipper or an international champion, somewhere in one of these categories you will find *your* reason for wanting to swim. Meanwhile learners and improvers can take heart from this fact: every top-class swimming and diving champion was once a non-swimmer and had to start at the shallow end.

More and more people are finding fun in other water sports too: canoeing, water skiing, dinghy sailing, skin diving and so on. To enjoy these sports to the full it is essential to be 'at home' in the water, and this means being able to swim.

WHERE TO LEARN

While it is possible to learn to swim in shallow sea water, or in a river or lake, the best place to learn is in the relaxed, safe and pleasant environment of the swimming pool. Here you will be able to relax and concentrate all your attention on making the right

Some swimming aids (like inflatable armbands and rings) you will be able to discard almost as soon as you can swim. Others (like floats, or kick boards) will still be used for kicking and pulling practice even when you have reached a very high standard of performance.

movements without having to keep an eye on tides, currents, wind, sharply shelving seabeds and so forth. There will also probably be someone at the pool to give you any help or advice you need.

GETTING OFF TO A GOOD START

Learning to swim should be a memorable and pleasant experience, not a penance performed in water, and the best way of making sure that your enjoyment is not spoiled is to get off to a good start.

Confidence is half the battle at the beginning, so give yourself all the help you can get from the various artificial aids now available. The best are inflatable rings and armbands, and polystyrene floats (or kick boards) which will give you extra buoyancy while you master the art of keeping your body more or less horizontal in the water. The rings and armbands you will soon discard but floats (or boards), which are especially useful in helping you to get the hang of the leg movements, will go on being useful even if you become a world-beating champion. So don't despise the idea of using an aid. Many a good stroke has been perfected with one, and many a bad habit broken. With the help of an aid, you can even be swimming after your first visit to the pool.

You can begin to make a swim enjoyable – for yourself and others – *before* you actually get into the pool. In the changing room make a point of folding or hanging your clothes neatly. Hand over money, watches or other valuables to the safekeeping of the attendant. Observe any special rules your particular pool makes; there will be a good reason for them. If you have long hair, tie it back or wear a bathing cap so that you will not be irritated or distracted by water running off it into your face.

Don't run, push or jostle at the poolside. And, once in the water, leave other swimmers enough room to continue their practice.

Check where the shallow end is and where you will be out of your depth. Even though you may be tempted to join more competent swimmers on the diving boards or having fun at the deep end, you must be quite a capable and confident swimmer before venturing there.

IMPROVE YOUR PERFORMANCE: KNOW-HOW

Knowing what to do next to improve is many a learner's problem. This book gives you a simple step-by-step guide that will take you from the first arm and leg movements, through the four major racing strokes and simple dives to survival swimming and life-saving. Whether you learn to swim on your own or receive at least one or two lessons, the information contained in these pages will improve your knowledge, and as your knowledge increases, so will your confidence and your skill. Remember, however, that no two people learn or improve at the same rate. So stick at it if you seem to make slow progress while some of your friends romp along. You may surprise them later.

The usual way of entering the pool is of course by diving in or jumping in, but until you feel completely at home and can control your body in the water, climb in *backwards* down the pool steps at the shallow end. If the area near the steps is crowded – and it often is – sit right on the edge with your legs dangling in the water and, holding the rail or side firmly, twist round on your hands and lower yourself into the water.

As soon as you are in, jump up and down quickly to help your body adjust to the slightly lower temperature of the water. Get your shoulders below the surface right away and start moving around; no-one ever learned to swim standing still.

Walk about the pool to get the feel of the water on your body. The best way is to take a step and then press backwards and to the sides with your hands, pulling your weight forward over your outstretched foot. This is the basic pulling principle used in the actual swimming strokes later.

Gradually move further into the pool (still at the shallow end) and then progress to jumping off the bottom and reaching for the rail, gutter or trough. If you keep your shoulders under the water surface you will find that your legs and feet will automatically lift behind you, taking your body more or less into the horizontal position required for swimming. You will also begin to feel that the water is actually holding you up.

If you are wearing an aid, now is the time to prove to yourself just how good it is in keeping you up at the surface. Push down on the aid with your hands and at the same time gently lift your feet off the bottom of the pool. Very soon you will realise that you can easily keep them up without any support. They can move about quite freely and, by making small circular movements with them, you can, when supported by your aid, turn round in circles. If your hands are also free they can be used to help the movement as well, and soon you will be spinning round in the water like a top. Then, by pushing with your hands and feet against the water, you will be able to move about in any direction you wish, with your aid keeping your head up and your mouth clear of the water so that you can breathe quite freely.

Sometimes at first it is just a little difficult to get back into an upright standing position. Practice is all that is needed. If you are lying on your back, lift your head out of the water and at the same time bend your knees, bringing your feet underneath you. By pushing down on the water with your hands, as though you were skipping backwards, you will become upright and able to reach down with your feet to touch the bottom.

Similarly, if you are lying on your front, bend your knees and push down with your hands and again, you will return to an upright position.

How to ge

GETTING YOUR HEAD UNDER

Every swimmer needs to get used to the feel of the water on his face. Begin by taking the water to your face, as if you were about to wash it. Then take your face to the water, holding your hands (palms upwards) just below the surface and dipping your face into the 'bowl'. Splash and pour water over your head and face in handfuls. Finally, duck your head right below the surface.

Once your head is under the water, open your eyes. Don't try to keep them open as they actually pass the surface; they will always automatically close at this point. And once you do open them, don't expect to see as clearly under water as you do above it. Your eyes will take time to adjust to the difference but keep practising until you are perfectly happy to sit on the bottom of the pool with your eyes wide open.

Any activity in the pool now will give you more

moving

confidence. So bob up and down, chase your friends about the shallow end, hold the rail or gutter and kick your legs, or tuck your feet behind it and move your arms about, lying face upwards. Pick up objects from the bottom of the pool. Every action will tell you *something* about the effect of the water on your movements.

At this stage the oftener you can visit the pool the faster your progress will be.

Floating, walking, sitting on the pool bottom – almost any activity will tell you *something* about moving about in the water and the effect it has on your body.

A good front float position: head down and in line with the swimmer's body, arms stretched well forward, and legs straight.

A bad front float position: the swimmer's head is poked up, his arms are too wide apart, and his legs have dropped.

The streamlined swimmer

Once you can move around easily with and without your aids you are ready to use your arms and legs to propel yourself across the pool, but before you do so, spare a thought for the position of your body as you swim. The designers of ships and planes give them streamlined shapes to increase their speed. Similarly, by giving your body a streamlined shape in the water you can improve *your* speed and efficiency.

Because we are two-legged creatures in the habit of walking upright most of the time, we find it difficult to change our head-up-seat-down position for a more horizontal one, even in the water. But a head-up-seat-down position offers a lot of resistance to the water and is therefore a bad position for swimming.

The greater the surface area of your body you present to the water ahead of you, the greater the resistance or drag you create, and the slower and harder it is to move. An experiment with a float (or kick board if it has one end larger than the other) will prove this. Push the float (or board) through the water with the broadest side or end leading. The pressure will build up against it as you push forward. Now repeat the experiment with the smaller side or end leading. It will now slip very easily through the water. In exactly the same way *you* will slip more easily through the water if you present a smaller body surface to the water ahead of you. To do this you must try to get a good flat, horizontal position in the water, with your head and legs kept closely in line with your body.

Again, you can put this to the test by pushing off from the side of the pool and gliding through the water in different positions:

1. Push off with your arms and hands stretched out in front of you, thumbs locked together.
2. Push off in the same position but this time stick your arms out to the side once you are under way. Your hands and arms now act as a resistance against the water and their braking effect will slow you down instantly.

A bad position on the back: the swimmer's head and shoulders are poked up and forward. This has caused his hips and feet to drop.

A good streamlined position on the back: the swimmer's head is well back, his arms are straight and fairly close to his sides, his legs are straight and his toes are pointed.

3. Try to find other ways in which your body resists the water and compare them with the most streamlined position you can find. You will soon be convinced that a long 'straight line' position is best.

The same streamlining idea applies when you swim on your back, but here the commonest fault is to bend in the middle with your seat lowered as if you were sitting in an armchair. Again, experiment by pushing off from the side to discover how much smoother and faster your glide is when you adopt the long streamlined shape.

THE POSITION OF YOUR HEAD

The position of your head in relation to the rest of your body also affects your position in the water: if your head is held poked up above the water your body will be forced into an incorrect upright position and your legs and feet will tend to hang down in the water. *The secret is to look in the right direction,* because it is the direction of your eyes that decides, more or less, the position of your head.

When you swim on your front you should look down at the bottom of the pool, not directly beneath you but a few yards ahead.

When you swim on your back, your head should be held in line with your body, not poked forward. Your chin should be tucked in and the water surface should just brush over your ears.

PUSH AND GLIDE

Practise pushing and gliding from the side of the pool on your back and front, applying the streamline principle. Try to travel further across the pool at each attempt, using the lines on the pool bottom to measure your progress.

Lie on the surface of the pool and make different shapes: a star, a ball, an arrow. Watch the effect these various floating positions have on your movement. You will learn a lot about the ideal position for swimming.

How and when to breathe

Above: practise blowing the air out hard and rhythmically with your face below the surface.

Below: practise the side-breathing action by turning your head just enough to get your mouth clear of the water. Keep your eyes open.

Although breathing is very important in good swimming because it provides the oxygen needed to put power into your muscles, it plays no part in the actual movement of your body through the water. Your breathing action should therefore interfere as little as possible with the movement of your legs and arms, and must be fitted in with their actions.

Breathing *out* presents more problems than breathing *in* for a learner. But once you have learned to breathe *out* correctly, you will have no difficulty getting the next breath *in.*

Right from the beginning all learners should practise blowing bubbles into the water by blowing hard through nose and mouth at the same time. Don't be too gentle about it, as the pressure of the water makes it quite difficult to force the air out under water. At first the best practice is to stand still in the water, take a good breath, immerse your face in the water and breathe out *powerfully*.

When you are accustomed to the breathing action, repeat it a number of times, jumping up and down in the water, ducking your face right below the surface. At first you will want to stop each time with your face and mouth *above* the surface, but with practice you will soon be able to bob up and down continuously. It then becomes very much easier to fit a correct breathing action into the swimming strokes, and the problem will become not so much *how* to breathe as *when* to breathe.

WHEN TO BREATHE

Ideally you should breathe in at the end of the major propelling movement of your hands and arms.

So, in *crawl stroke,* you breathe in *when one arm is just completing a pull and the other is just about to start its pull.* Your head is turned to one side (whichever side you prefer) and your mouth clears the water just enough to allow the exchange of air to take place. Again, this movement can be practised while you stand still and lean forward with your head in the water, or do kick practices with a float (or board).

In *breast stroke* and *butterfly* you breathe in *at the end of the arm pull, with your head facing forwards* and lifted only very slightly – just enough to let you make the change of air.

In *back crawl* it is obviously much easier to breathe because your mouth is clear of the water throughout the stroke.

In the early stages of learning the strokes you will find it very useful to hold your breath for short spells while you concentrate on the arm and leg actions. But it very soon becomes vital to make sure that you make a regular and complete change of breath, usually once in each stroke cycle.

Breast stroke

Breathe in towards the end of the arm pull *with your head facing forward* and raised very slightly, but held steady without any bobbing.

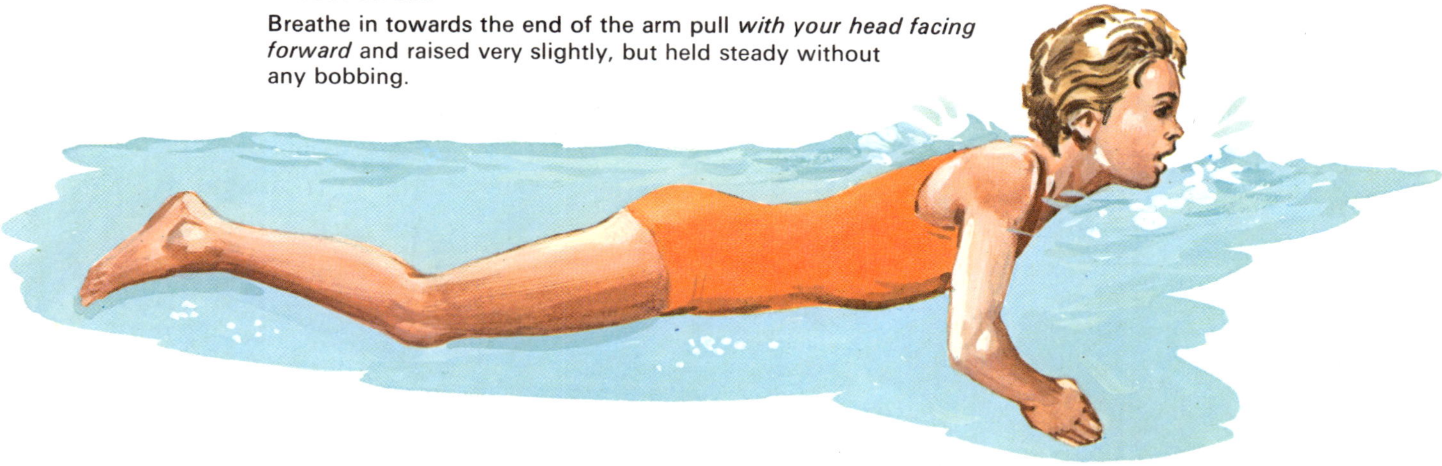

Front crawl

Breathe in *with your head turned to one side*, just as one arm finishes its pull and the other begins its pull.

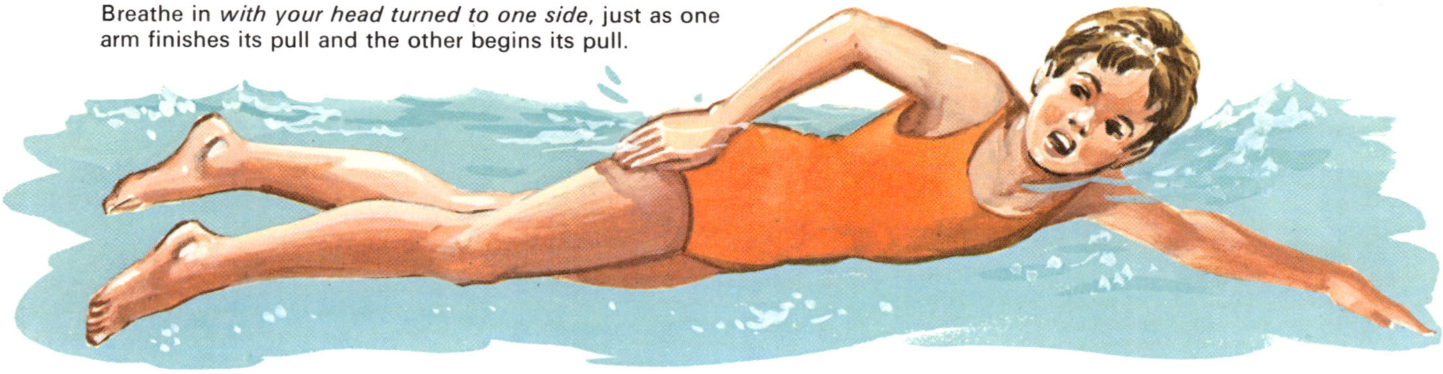

Butterfly

Again, breathe in at the end of the arm pull, *with your head facing forward* and lifted slightly up and back.

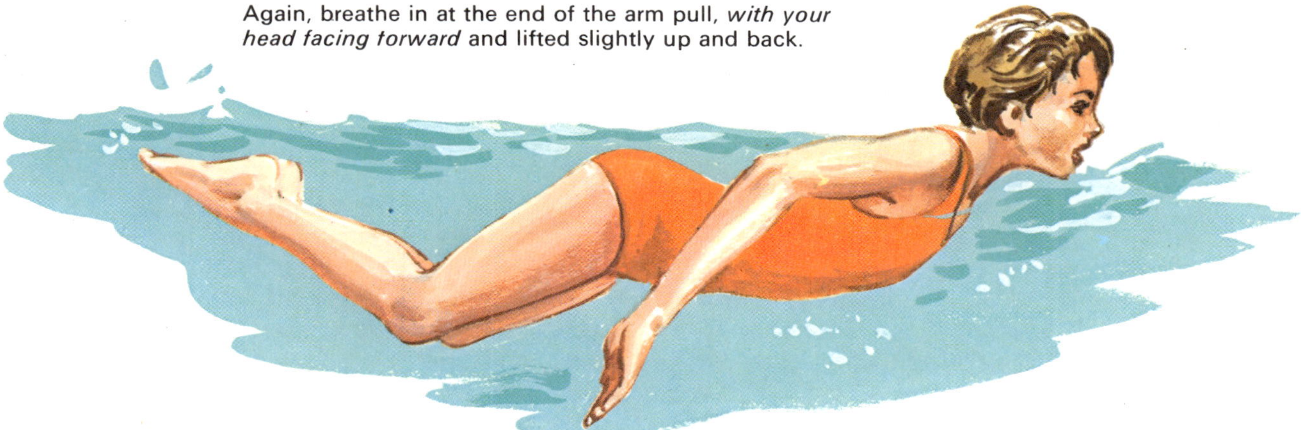

Back crawl

Although your mouth is always clear of the water in back crawl, you should breathe in at this point in each arm cycle, just as one arm is about to come to the end of its pull.

Legs and feet: the basic kicks

Although the first temptation is to use your arms to *pull* yourself along, it is much better to learn first how to propel yourself with your feet and legs. This is because, as you have already seen, your legs and the lower part of your body tend to sink towards the pool bottom and upset your streamlined position. To overcome this you must kick against the water to keep them up near the surface. It is also easier later on to make the correct arm movements if you have a good drive coming from your 'rear engine'.

There are two basic kicks: the *crawl kick* and the *breast stroke kick.* No matter which you find easiest at first you should learn and practise both, using a float (or board) until you get the actions right.

For practising on your front, hold the float (or board) ahead of you with arms outstretched, gripping it at the sides but with fingers underneath and thumbs on top.

For practising on your back, use the same grip but hold your thumbs against your chest so that the float (or board) lies above you.

Now hold two floats (or boards), one under each arm, and try to repeat the same movement you practised at the rail. It is best to start with a good push and glide. Then try to keep yourself moving along.

THE CRAWL OR FLUTTER KICK

This is done by moving your feet *vertically* (up and down) near the surface of the water. Whether this kick is done on your back or your front, and whether you kick your feet alternately, or hold them together and move them up and down simultaneously like a fish tail, you must make sure of the following points if your body is to move forward:

1. Feet must be kept long and pointed.
2. Knees must bend only very slightly.
3. The kick must start right at the top of the leg and near the hips.
4. Heels (in front crawl) and toes (in back crawl) should break the surface with a slight splash.
5. Knees and ankles should not be held too tense and stiff as this will produce a very small, shallow kick that is of little use in propelling you forward and is tiring to your leg muscles.

PRACTISING THE CRAWL KICK

When you practise the crawl kick remember to keep your feet long and pointed, and splash them both up and down in a continuous rhythm. Holding a float (or board) ahead of you, kick yourself across the pool, one width with your face in the water, the next with your head looking straight in front, and so on.

Breast stroke kick

Kick both legs at the same time, with feet pulled up short and flat and turned outwards during the thrust backwards. Let your heels lead the thrust.

Crawl kick

Kick your legs alternately up and down. Your feet should be kept long and pointed, with your heels just breaking the surface. The kick should not be a deep one – not much deeper than the depth of your body is about right.

Dolphin kick

This is an up and down kick that is similar to the crawl kick but with both legs performing the action at the same time. Your toes are kept long and pointed and your feet should be held together all through the kick.

A COMMON FAULT IN BACK CRAWL KICK

The back crawl kick is very similar to the front crawl kick except that there is always a tendency for the swimmer's knees to bend more. This is a bad fault and every effort must be made to splash with your feet without letting your knees break the surface at any time.

THE BREAST STROKE OR FROG KICK

In the *crawl kick* the swimmer's legs act one after the other (alternately, that is). In the *breast stroke kick* both legs act simultaneously, that is, they both make the same movement at the same time.

Despite its name, the breast stroke kick can be done on the back as well as the front. And as its alternative name, *frog kick*, suggests, you bend your knees to draw your feet up to your seat, and in this crouched kind of position you pull your feet up *short and flat* before pushing round and backwards against the water with the soles and insides of your feet. The backwards push of the kick propels you forward and it is therefore very important to perform it correctly.

A COMMON FAULT IN BREAST STROKE KICK

Many swimmers never do a really good breast stroke kick because when they draw up their feet in preparation for it they also tend to draw up their thighs closer to their bodies. This acts against the streamlining position described on page 10. So when you draw the lower part of your legs into the knees-bent position try to restrict the movement of your thighs to an absolute minimum so that they move only very slightly nearer to your body.

THE SECRET OF THE BREAST STROKE KICK

The real secret of a good breast stroke kick lies in pulling your feet up *short and flat, and turned out to the side* (as shown in the top drawing above) before you make the backward push. Try the movement while sitting on the edge of the pool with your legs dangling in the water. Watch your feet carefully, and pause in the knees-bent position to check that your feet point out to the sides. Then push, with your heels leading, as you straighten your legs. Keep your heels apart except when your legs are fully stretched.

Next, but with float (or board) in front of you, try the movement in the water on your back and then on your front. As long as you flatten your feet and turn them outwards to kick, you will move steadily along with each kick. When you can complete a full width of the pool, count the number of kicks you take and then begin to cut it down. The fewer kicks you need, the better you are performing each one.

An all-too-common fault is to kick with one foot stretched and the other pulled up short in the proper position. If you do not correct this fault quite early then you will be left with the dreaded 'screw kick'. It is better to avoid this but if you find that you do have one, don't despair. It can be corrected if you concentrate on the correct foot position.

Dog paddle: press backwards under your body with the flat palm of one hand while the other slides forward under your chin ready to take over the pull.

Arms and hands: sculling and dog paddle

After learning to keep a good streamlined position and practising the different leg kicks, the next step is to begin to use your hands and arms to propel you through the water.

You use them in much the same way that you would use a canoe paddle, applying the largest surface available (your flattened hand in swimming) to exert pressure against the water in the direction *opposite* that in which you want to move.

Earlier you saw how to overcome the pressure of the water and pull yourself easily over your feet by pressing backwards with your arms (*see* page 8). This is the basis of all movement, both in the water and out of it. The main difference is that whereas the earth provides a runner's feet with a firm resistance against which he can exert force, water offers no such grip to a swimmer's hands, and there is a good deal of 'slipping'. The effect is similar to running up a sandhill. If the runner's feet are carelessly placed, they will slip backwards in the sand, but if they are sensitively placed they will gain just enough hold (or resistance) to lift his body up the sandhill. In the same way, a swimmer must learn to treat the water gently, pressing carefully rather than tearing at it with his hands and fingers in order to move himself forward.

Sculling and dog paddling are two practices which help you to develop this skill of getting a gentle grip on the water.

SCULLING

This is best done lying on your back, as shown in the illustration opposite. With arms held quite close to your sides, your hands make a small circular movement, rotating clockwise from your wrists. During the *push* phase your palms face towards your feet, and during the *passive*, or inactive, phase when your wrists are being rotated backwards for the next pull, they slip round so that they face the bottom of the pool.

At first it is easier to practise sculling while wearing a lightly inflated ring. Later on, when your back crawl kick is stronger you can fit it in with the sculling action of your hands to keep you up at the surface.

DOG PADDLE: ALTERNATING ARMS

Done on your front, this teaches you to use your hands well in the water. As its name suggests, you move your hands like the paws of a swimming dog, first one and then the other, in a circular movement under your chin and chest. The movement is a fairly short one, with each arm at first making only a very short pull. Very soon you can begin to lengthen the pull underneath your body.

After the longer arm pull, you will then find that the best way of getting your hands back to the front again ready for their next pull is to swing them right out and over the water surface. You will use this circular windmilling action for front crawl stroke later, but at this stage just concentrate on keeping your head steady and moving your arms *continuously*. Don't try to fit a breath in and you will find that you can swim as much as ten yards like this before having to stop to breathe.

You will also find that you have a tendency to swim too fast. Relax, and try not to do this. Just try to fit a good, steady kick to a streamlined position.

DOG PADDLE: DOUBLE ARM ACTION

Some learners prefer to keep their heads up and out of the water. For them the dog paddle done with both arms performing the same movement at the same time is probably best, but with the movement kept very short and in front of the face – used more to keep the swimmer's head out of the water to get a good breath than to propel him forward.

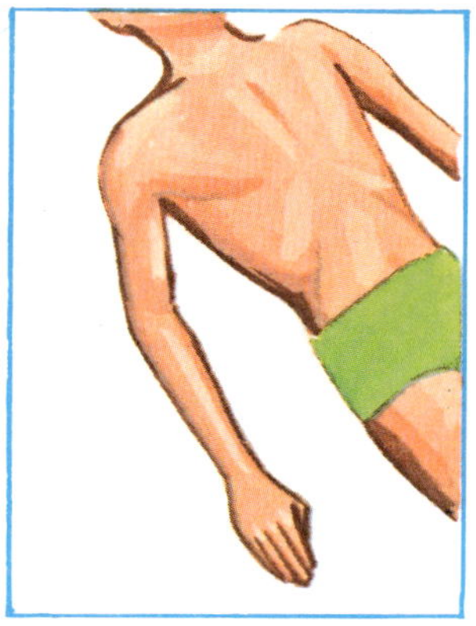

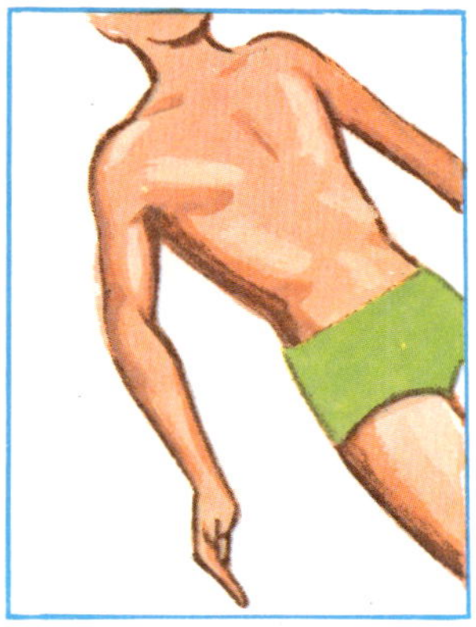

Sculling: lie on your back in a good streamlined position with your arms fairly close to your sides. Now make small circular clockwise movements with your hands, first pushing with your palms facing forwards towards your feet, and then letting them slip backwards facing the bottom of the pool, little finger first.

The double-arm action will later be used as the basis for breast stroke and butterfly, and with this movement it is even more vital than in the crawl to have a good strong and correct leg kick.

HOW TO MAKE YOUR ARMS EFFICIENT
Five main things make your arm movements in the water efficient or inefficient: (1) the size of the surface area pushing against the water, (2) the direction of your hand movement, (3) the length of your arm movement, (4) the power of the movement, and (5) timing and continuity.

The size of the pushing surface. Obviously you cannot increase the actual size of your hand. But you can make sure that you use it as efficiently as possible. Avoid any tendency to cup your hand, and at the same time take care not to open your fingers wide and allow the water to slip between them.

Another quite common fault is to allow the propelling surface to 'give way' at the wrist or elbow. This is rather like trying to row a boat with an oar fitted with a hinge that folds back as soon as it meets pressure from the water. So keep the 'hinges' of your wrists and elbows firmly fixed during the propelling phases.

The direction of your hand movement. Your body will move in the direction opposite to that in which you exert the pressure on the water. For example, to travel forwards, you must push backwards towards your feet. It is interesting to experiment by pressing in different directions and watching the effect this has on your movement.

The length of your arm movement. A very short press will produce only a little movement, whereas a longer one will produce greater movement. The longer one, however, brings with it a problem: the problem of recovery, or how to bring your hand back to the starting point for its next pull. A bad recovery reduces your forward movement. So read carefully the descriptions of the *correct* recovery techniques for each of the four racing strokes.

The power of your arm movement. Again this will obviously depend to a great extent on how strong your shoulder and chest muscles are, but you can make sure that you put whatever power you do have to the best possible use. If you had to scale a wall or climb a rope you would keep your hands and arms quite close to your body in order to apply all your strength in the best possible way. The same idea of 'keeping compact' applies in the water, and you will see how to do so in the chapters on the actual swimming strokes. When you apply your strength correctly and efficiently in the water, a kind of *pull/push* action results.

Timing and continuity. The best way to pull yourself through the water is to keep up a constant pressure on it all the time. This is extremely difficult to do, especially when you have to fit your breathing into the pattern of movements as well.

The crawl stroke demonstrates the *pull/push* action best because there is almost always one arm pushing backwards at any given moment in the stroke, whereas in breast stroke there is a moment when no pressure at all is being applied.

In front crawl as one arm comes towards the end of its pull the other is about to enter the water. The fingers enter first, followed by the wrist and – last of all – by the elbow. Your head should be kept in line with your body, eyes open and looking forward and down. Legs kick alternately up and down.

Front crawl

The smooth, efficient strokes that mark a good swimmer are the result of the correct combination of body position, leg kick, arm action, breathing, and correct timing. In the following pages these five important elements of the four racing strokes (front crawl, back crawl, breast stroke and dolphin butterfly) will be explained in detail.

Front crawl is the fastest of all the swimming strokes because the propelling force is applied almost without a break, first by one arm and then by the other. Any small break that does occur in the arm action is bridged by the movement produced by the swimmer's legs.

Front crawl is faster than back crawl because the powerful chest and shoulder muscles are used to greater advantage.

BODY POSITION
Your body should always be as flat and horizontal in the water as possible, and your head should be kept in line with your body. The water should cut your head just around the hairline, although it may be slightly lower or higher for a swimmer who is much more or less buoyant than average.

Look forwards and downwards to the bottom of the pool as you swim, not straight ahead. The lines of the pool bottom will help you to keep moving in a straight line.

Rolling. As your stroke improves you will find that your arm and shoulder action will be better and your breathing made easier if you let your body rotate slightly round your spine.

Do not confuse rotation with the snaking action that is caused if you allow your shoulders and arms to swing too much. This causes the body to sway from side to side and prevents you from having a really good arm pull.

LEG KICK
In front crawl the leg kick has three functions to perform:

1. It helps to keep the heavy, lower end of your body up near the surface.
2. It counteracts the sideways swinging of your body caused by your arm action.
3. When required, it helps to propel you forward during any blank phase in your arm pull.

The front crawl kick is an *alternating vertical action:* as your left leg kicks up, your right leg drops back, and vice versa. Your feet are extended and your toes are kept pointed away from your body.

The kick starts at the top of the thigh and your knee is kept *straight,* especially during the *up* kick. Only your heels should break the surface with a light splash. But many swimmers kick much more vigorously, especially when they are sprinting fast.

The *down* kick should not be deeper than a few inches below your body level. If it goes deeper than that, it will reduce your speed.

ARM ACTION: THE MAIN PROPELLING FORCE
When they are correctly used your arms are the main propelling force in front crawl. Like your legs, they act alternately: while your right arm is active and pulling, your left is recovering, and vice versa.

The arm action is easier to understand if it is broken down into three phases: *entry, pull* and *recovery.*

Entry. This is the phase at which the swimmer's hand is put into the water ready to make its pull, and should be done in a controlled manner without slapping the water surface. The point of entry is in front of the head.

The order of entry to remember is:

FINGERS – WRIST – ELBOW

Your fingers cut into the water first, followed by

front crawl action

1. The swimmer's right hand enters in a controlled manner (fingers first), when the left arm is mid-way through its pull.
The right knee is slightly bent, heel at the surface.

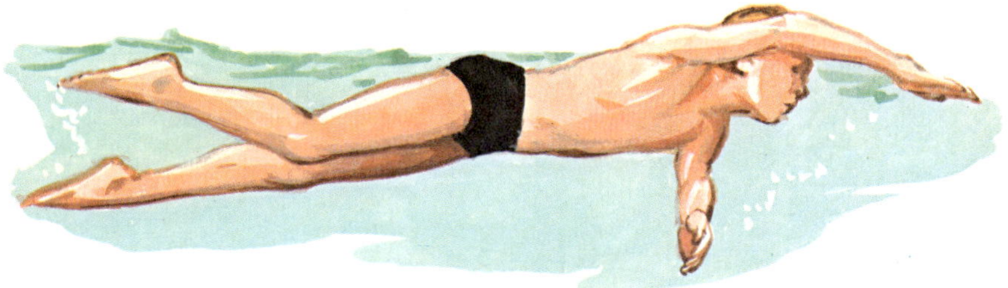

2. The right arm presses back and down. The left arm begins its recovery, and the elbow starts to bend.
The left leg is kicking down vigorously, balancing the powerful right arm action.

3. Now mid-way through its pull, the right arm keeps a high elbow position. The left elbow is now well bent and also lifted high.
The right ankle is well pointed to press on the water. The left heel is just breaking the surface.

4. As the right arm completes its pull, the swimmer's head starts to turn as he is breathing out.
The left ankle here shows excellent flexibility. The right leg is straight as it kicks up.

5. After the breath has been taken, the head begins to return to the front. Note the 'boomerang' shape of the arm and how the left hand presses firmly backwards.
The feet pass close together at this stage.

6. The sequence of the arm movements is now complete and the right arm is ready to begin the next cycle.
The legs too have completed their 6-beat cycle.

Front crawl recovery

The ideal arm recovery position with elbow lifted high to bring your hand through in a fast but relaxed manner.

Front crawl entry

Your elbow is still kept lifted, allowing your fingers to enter the water first, followed by your wrist. This places your hand perfectly for the pull.

Front crawl pull

The swimmer on the right has the better pull, with a *bent* arm that is pulling down and under his body. The swimmer on the left has a weaker position: his pulling hand is slipping sideways and will cause too much body swing.

A slight rotation of your body round your spine just as each arm is about to start pulling brings the strong muscles of your chest and back into powerful action in front crawl. It also helps to lift your recovery arm well clear of the water.

your wrist and, last of all, by your elbow. The elbow joint should always be kept slightly bent to make sure that you have a strong pulling position.

Pull. From their slightly bent entry position in front of your head, your hand and forearm press down and begin to pull backwards in a path that more or less follows the mid-line of your body, but with a slight movement outwards from the mid-line at the start of the pull, back towards the centre in mid-pull, and finally out again at the end of the pull. This slightly *s*-shaped path of your pulling hand should never be allowed to become a slicing action, as backward pressure on the water will then be lost. And it is the backward pressure that sends you forward.

The length of the arm pull varies with speed and the strength of the pulling muscles (For example, boys usually have a stronger arm pull than girls.) In general, however, it is advisable to continue the pull right under your body until your hand is level with your thigh.

During the pulling phase imagine that you are swimming through a long, narrow tube, and keep your hands close to your body as you swim.

Recovery. When your arm has completed its pull, it must be lifted over the water surface back to the point of entry. The recovery movement does not help to propel you forward, but it is an important phase in the stroke all the same, and must be performed carefully and in time with the opposite pulling arm so that it does not upset your streamlined body position.

A bent-elbow recovery, in which you lift your elbow high, bringing hand and arm clear of the water, is best. The hand can then be brought forward almost in a straight line to the point of entry.

Avoid a straight-arm recovery. Try to think of your arm as a boomerang shape to help get the action right.

BREATHING

The basic breathing action was explained on page 12.

The important thing to remember is that you must make a full and regular exchange of breath without interfering with the propelling movements of your arms and legs. The only suitable moment for this in front crawl is when one arm has just completed its pull and the other hand has just entered the water ready to begin its pull. The top illustration opposite shows how the swimmer's head turns just enough to bring his mouth clear of the water.

An expert swimmer makes the exchange of breath while his mouth is actually just below the true level of the water, behind the bow wave created by his head.

Every swimmer has a favourite side for breathing to but you should be able to breathe to left or right.

TIMING

To perform a good crawl stroke your arm and leg movements must be as continuous as possible. This can be achieved with a variety of styles. Some swimmers kick their legs continuously with six leg beats to each complete arm cycle, while others will do only four or even as few as two kicks to an arm cycle. And many just allow their legs to drag along behind and do a kind of cross-over kick. Some swimmers have a fast arm action, whereas others lean on their arms longer. None of these variations is in itself either 'right' or 'wrong' as long as the stroke is made in a basically correct way and does not upset either the streamlining or the continuous action.

FRONT CRAWL PRACTICES

The practices in the chapter about feet and legs (page 14), arms and hands (page 16), and breathing (page 12) are, of course, extremely useful but once you can perform the basic actions, you must set to work to improve the stroke over a longer distance. For this the *sectional practices* in kicking and pulling that are described on page 42 are best.

In back crawl your head and the upper part of your body act as a firm base for your arms to pull from. This swimmer shows a perfect position just before the entry of her left hand

Back crawl

In back crawl the swimmer's nose and mouth are always above the surface and there is therefore no breathing problem. For this reason back crawl is preferred by many swimmers. This does not mean that it takes less skill to perform than the other strokes. At the highest level of performance it has been described as front crawl swum on the back, because as in front crawl the leg kick is both vertical and alternating (the left leg kicking while the right leg recovers).

BODY POSITION

You must have a good body position for an efficient back crawl, especially in the early stages of learning the stroke. So attention to the push and glide practices on page 11 will pay well later.

Your body needs to be held flat and streamlined in the water, lying just *below* the surface, not actually on it. Take care to avoid the common fault of letting your hips drop into a sitting position. At the same time avoid too much tension in your body. Only your face and part of your head should be above the water, although when you are swimming very fast, your chest and part of your shoulders will appear above the surface from time to time.

HEAD POSITION

In back crawl the position of your head is all-important and will be decided by the point on which you fix your gaze. Ideally it should be held well back in the water and in line with your body, but as this usually causes water to flow over your face and eyes, it is better to look up at an angle of about 60° from your body, fixing your gaze on a suitable point in the roof – or on a tree or diving tower in an outdoor pool. It is *vital* that your head should not roll from side to side.

LEG KICK

Although the back crawl kick is in some ways similar to the front crawl kick, there are some differences. A really good leg kick is of much more importance in back crawl than in front.

The back crawl leg kick is *a vertical alternating movement* in which your feet pass each other closely, with toes extended. Loose and flexible ankles are essential and are a characteristic of all great back-stroke swimmers. You kick slightly deeper than in front crawl, but only your toes should break the surface at the height of the kick.

A major fault seen in almost all swimmers learning back crawl is their tendency to bend their knees in a kind of cycling action so that they keep appearing above the surface. Avoid this right from the start and never let it occur again. Concentrate on stretching your legs out as far as you can and kicking with the upper borders of your feet to remove this fault.

Keeping your leg action *continuous* is also vital in back crawl, even when your arms are working at full power.

back crawl action

1. The left arm enters the water with little finger first, arm straight and close beside the head.
   The left knee, although slightly bent, does not break the surface during the up kick.

2. Left arm, now in the water, begins to pull. It remains straight until it reaches shoulder level. The recovery arm is lifted clear of the water, with the back of the hand facing upwards.
   The left foot, toes pointed, makes a splash, and the right foot is at its deepest point.

3. The left arm, now past shoulder level in its pull, bends at the elbow and *pushes* towards the feet. The recovery arm is held high and straight.
   The feet pass close to each other.

4. As the left arm completes its pull (with the hand facing palm downwards) the right arm enters the water.
   The left leg is pushing down towards the bottom of the pool.

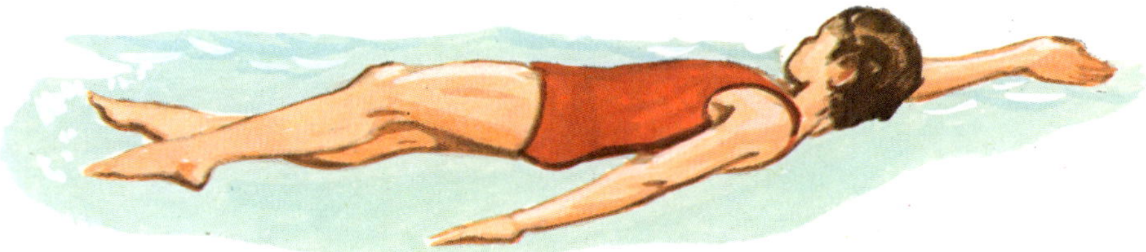

5. The right arm now begins its pull. Notice the slight rotation of the body round the spine. Despite this, the head should be kept perfectly still. (This swimmer's head has swung round with the rotation; this is bad and should be avoided.)
   The left leg is balancing the stretch of the right hand and arm. The right knee is near but just below the surface.

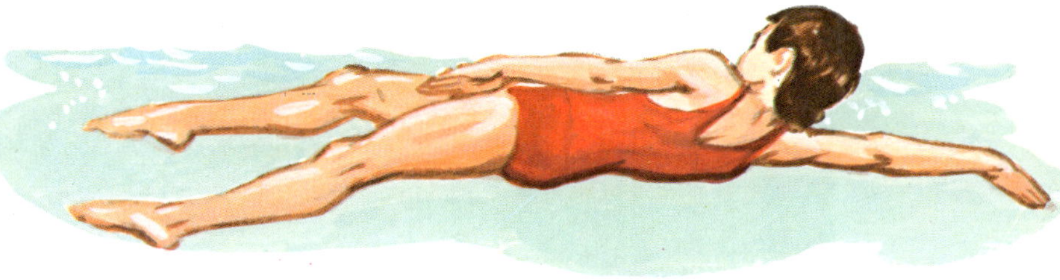

6. As the left arm (still kept straight) nears the end of the recovery, the right arm has almost completed its pull.
   The legs have now almost returned to the position shown in Phase 1, having completed their 6-beat cycle.

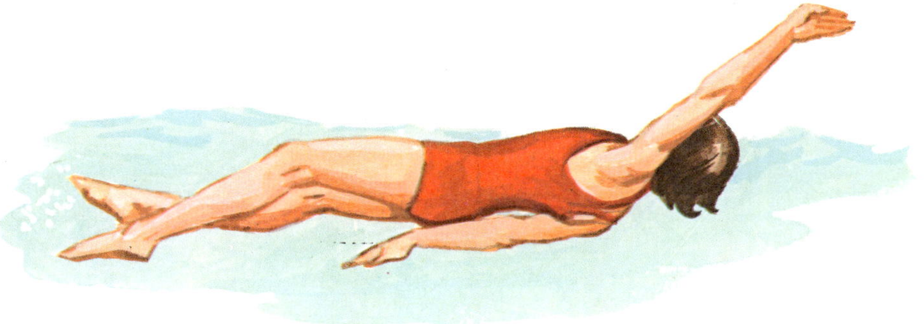

ARM ACTION

Although the leg kick plays an important part in back crawl, it is your arms that provide the main propelling force, just as they do in front crawl.

Entry. This is made beyond your head with your arm completely straight and as close to your ears as possible. The actual point of entry will be determined by the suppleness of your shoulders but as most young swimmers are reasonably flexible, achieving the right position is not difficult.

Again, a carefully controlled entry is important, with your wrist and arm rotated so that your little finger enters the water first, palm facing away from your body. *This is one of the few occasions in swimming when you keep your elbow quite straight,* and even here it remains straight only until the rest of your arm is in the water. The entry should be performed very carefully and deliberately, almost to the point of exaggerating it.

Pull. This is no longer done as a shallow, straight-arm movement but much more as a two-phase *pull-push* action. Your arm, straight on entry, begins to pull towards your feet. As soon as possible your upper arm rotates, causing your elbow to bend slightly. This bend increases but your elbow must remain *behind* your hand, not in front of it. Your hand and forearm are now used as a paddle to push backwards on the water towards your feet, as shown in the *illustration opposite.* From this mid-point your hand and wrist continue pushing but they also rotate, so that at the end of the movement alongside your thigh your palm faces the bottom of the pool.

This last phase is done *fast*, and has to be emphasised to prevent your hand from slicing out of the water too soon.

A real danger with this modern pull is that your elbow will lead the movement, preventing your hand and forearm from achieving maximum pressure on the water. This must be avoided.

To make the pull even stronger, your shoulders should roll from side to side around the spine. During this dipping action, however, *your head must remain absolutely steady.*

Recovery. At the end of the pull, your arm is completely straight and alongside your thigh, and the back of your hand is facing upwards. It is then easy to lift your wrist, keeping your arm straight but relaxed, and swing it right over your body and head, back to the entry position.

If you make the recovery swing too near the centre of your body, water may drop into your eyes, upsetting both your concentration and your steady body position. This can be avoided by making your recovery slightly wider.

Pushing off from the side of the pool is an exciting way to begin swimming back crawl.

BREATHING

This should present no problem at all, as your mouth is always clear of the water in back crawl. But in the early learning stages you may have a tendency to hold your breath too long. *Exchange your breath once every stroke cycle,* preferably at the same point each time, *towards the end of one arm pull and just before the start of the next.*

TIMING

There are fewer variations of style in the back crawl than in any of the other strokes, and these usually depend on how good the swimmer's leg kick is. The most important points to aim for are:

1. *Continuity in the leg kick.*
2. *Controlled entry of your hand, with a fast final push and immediate recovery of the hand when it reaches thigh level.*

PRACTICE FOR BACK CRAWL

1. *Push and glide:* check that your body position and head position are good.

2. *Leg kick:* with float (or board) held to your chest; with float (or board) held with arms stretched beyond your head; without float (or board), palms together, wrists twisted, arms beyond your head, elbows straight.

3. *Arm pull:* single-arm pulling action on back and side; double-arm simultaneous pulling; alternate arm pulling with a float (or board) between your legs.

4. *Full stroke:* concentrating on any points which you know are your particular weaknesses.

Above: back crawl start of recovery
The recovery arm is lifted out of the water and swung back in a relaxed manner, with the wrist and the back of the hand facing upwards. The elbow is kept straight.

Left: back crawl mid-pull
In mid-pull the pulling arm (the left in this illustration) is bent. What began as a *pulling* action now becomes a *pushing* action, with the hand and forearm pressing directly towards the feet.

Below: back crawl mid-recovery
As the recovery arm continues its swing, the wrist begins to rotate. This turns the hand out ready for entry. The elbow is still kept straight.

Back crawl entry
The arm is held close to the head, with the wrist now fully turned so that the palm faces away from the swimmer's body, and the little finger goes into the water first.

Breast stroke

Breast stroke, or at least a version of it, was the original stroke used in competitive swimming. And it was the stroke used by Captain Webb, the first man to swim the English Channel, in 1875. Over the years there have been many changes in it, some of them quite dramatic, including the introduction of an over-the-surface recovery action (now barred) from which the butterfly stroke finally evolved.

In the 1950s breast stroke was in danger of disappearing almost completely from view when swimmers found that they could go faster by swimming it completely underwater. The swimming laws were, however, changed and now at least part of the swimmer's head must be held above the surface, except for one complete stroke cycle allowed under water after the start and after turns in competitive events.

BODY POSITION

Although some swimmers prefer breast stroke because it can be swum with the head held high and the face and mouth clear of the water, this is a very bad position. Your head should be held in line with your body, especially during the powerful leg drive. However, if your head is held a little higher than this, it should be kept as steady as possible. Any excessive bobbing action upsets your body streamlining.

THE LEG KICK

The breast stroke kick has changed a lot in the past few years. When it was realised that the best way of moving forwards was by pushing *backwards* on the water, the kick changed from the old *wedge-type kick* to a faster, narrower *whip-type movement.* From the stretched position with the toes pointed for streamlining, the swimmer's knees bend, bringing his feet close up to his seat, but without bringing his thighs upwards and closer to his body. When the knees are

The stretch position: this is held only for a second or two at the end of the leg kick. Your whole body should be kept streamlined to make the most of the thrust from the kick, and your hands should be turned out ready to pull before the impetus is lost.

breast stroke action

1. *Stretch position:* arms straight and hands turned ready to pull. Head down but with part showing above surface. Legs and feet stretched.

2. *Mid-pull:* the elbows are kept high while the hands and forearms circle round and backwards to shoulder level. Legs are still kept straight.

3. *Breathing:* the head is raised while the breath is taken at the end of the arm pull. Legs have just started to bend in preparation for the kick.

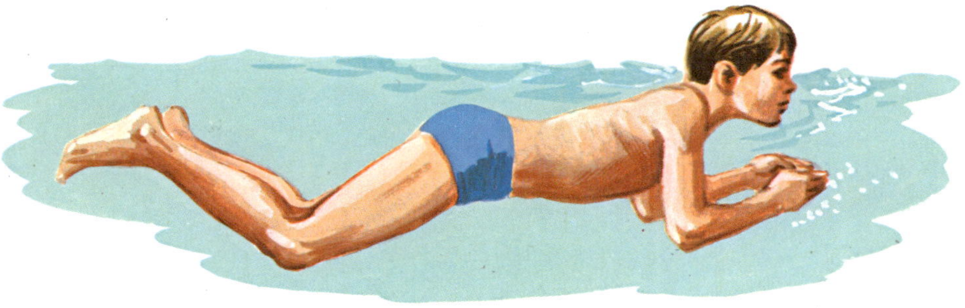

4. In breast stroke the hands are always kept ahead of the swimmer's face. Here they are ready to stretch forward. Elbows are kept in a compact line. Toes are still pointed back but the legs are now bent more sharply towards the seat.

5. *The leg drive:* from the knees-bent position the feet (held flat and turned out) are driven round and back. This is the powerful action that propels the swimmer forward. Arms are almost fully stretched.

6. *The glide:* the powerful leg kick takes the swimmer into a glide in the long, stretched position ready to repeat the whole cycle of movements over again.

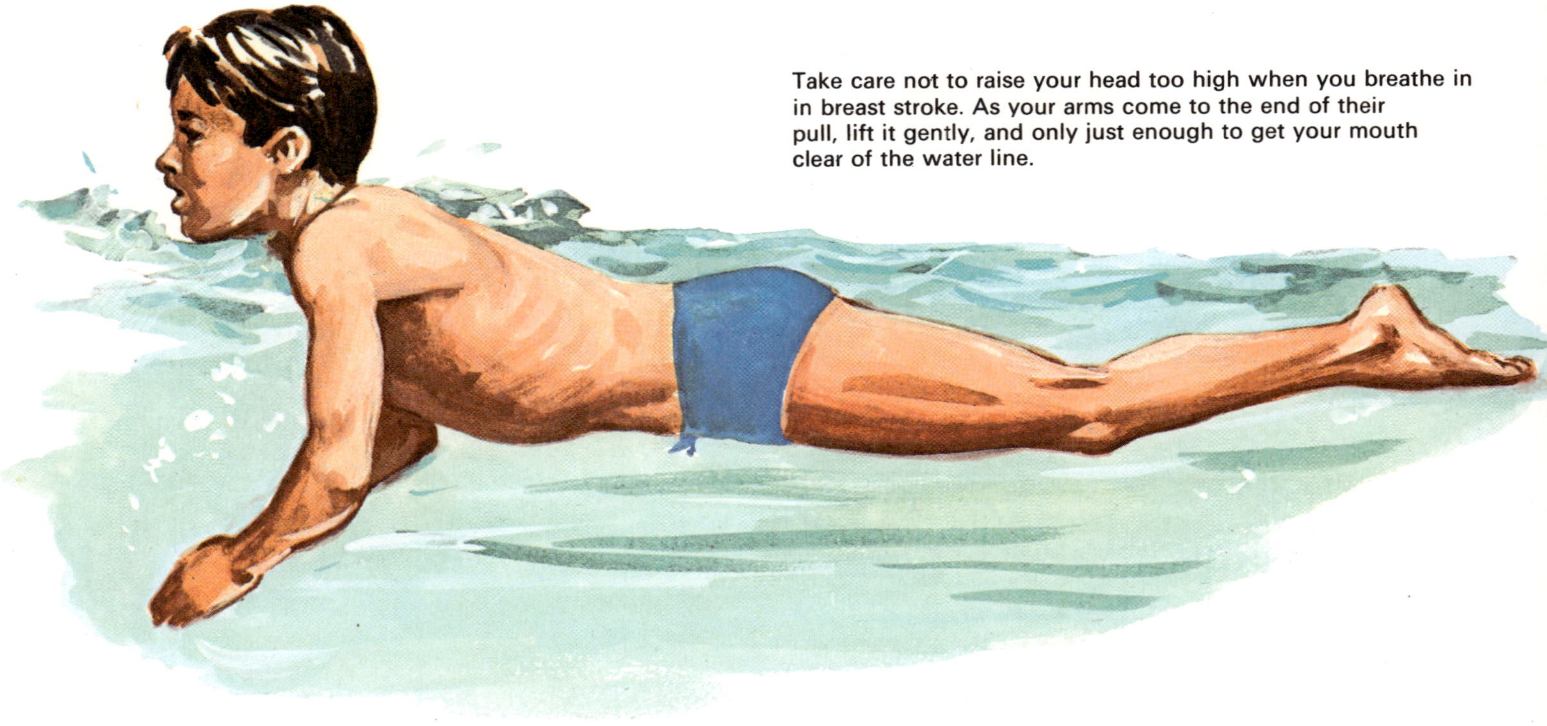

Take care not to raise your head too high when you breathe in in breast stroke. As your arms come to the end of their pull, lift it gently, and only just enough to get your mouth clear of the water line.

bent, just before the backward straightening movement, the feet must be:

pulled up short, toes towards the knees
turned out to the side, with heels apart.

Your knees should be kept fairly close together, and certainly not stuck out to the sides. From this position the strong whip-like action is started. Your heels lead the movement round and backwards with the soles and insides of your feet pressing on the water until your legs are completely straight and together.

This modern breast stroke kick can be a little difficult to master but concentration on the following points and practice will soon bring improvement:

1. Knees fairly close together and not bent too much under the body.
2. Feet slightly wider apart than the knees, and turned out.
3. Heels lead the kick and push backwards.

It can sometimes be helpful to try to visualise the shape that your heels are making as they kick. Try to think of them making a 'U' shape rather than an 'O'. This may help to improve your kick.

ARM ACTION

Although in the early stages it may be useful to keep your head up to enable you to breathe, once you have developed a good leg kick your arms should also help to propel you forward.

From the fully stretched position shown in the illustration, the arm movement is round and backwards, with your elbows held high, as in front crawl, to make a circle with your hands. It should not be a weak movement but a powerful *push* on the water, and the circle should not be so far back that it takes the hands behind the line of your shoulders. It is best if the whole arm movement takes place in front of your face. If your hands are drawn further back, your unsupported head and shoulders will drop and a bobbing action will result. The most critical phase of the arm pull is therefore towards the end when your hands must be brought in under your chin. This is done by rotating your wrists and forearms inwards. Your elbows will follow but should not be brought in too close to your chest. From this curled position your hands are stretched forward under the surface close together and palms facing downwards (not together as in prayer).

BREATHING

In the older versions of the breast stroke the breath was taken at the start of the arm action, thus making the arm pull less effective. Now, in the modern version, the breath is delayed until your arms have almost completed their pull and are almost into the recovery phase. At this point your head is lifted upwards just far enough for your mouth to clear the surface, the breath is taken in, and then your head is dropped back to its original position. The less this action interferes with a steady position the better. The breath should be blown out explosively into the water just before you lift your head.

TIMING

Because in breast stroke the actions of legs, arms and breathing are almost independent of each other, this is the most difficult of the four racing strokes to co-ordinate well. Aim to make the propelling action as continuous as possible, establishing a good rhythm of

KICK – PULL – BREATHE
KICK – PULL – BREATHE

The start of the kick: the most important position in breast stroke. Avoid pulling your knees too far underneath your body, and try to keep your horizontal, streamlined position in the water.

Inset: in the fully bent position your feet should be turned well out, with knees no more than hip width apart.

The only point when the action is not continuous is when you are in the fully stretched position, when the stretch is held for a second to give you most benefit from the forward glide from the leg kick.

At the end of the arm pull, while the breath is being taken and before your legs have started into their recovery, it is important to keep your hands moving continuously.

BREAST STROKE PRACTICE: KICKING

1. On the back, keeping knees under the surface and hands held over head.
2. On front – kick with knees held closely together.
3. On front – thumbs locked together, raise head to breathe just before each kick.

BREAST STROKE PRACTICE: PULLING

1. Standing in the water at chest height, bend chin forward on surface. Begin with a small circular hand and wrist action, then gradually extend it to include the forearm. Bring in the upper arm as well, but keep elbows up throughout.
2. With a float (or board) held between the legs. Again start with a small action, then gradually increase it.
3. With different leg kicks, e.g. front crawl, and dolphin.

VARIATIONS

There are probably more variations of the breast stroke than of any other stroke. It would be wrong therefore to say that any one version of it is 'correct' and the others wrong. Even among the world's greatest swimmers there is quite a wide range of styles. Such differences in style are usually the result of different physiques and body shapes. A lean swimmer with long legs usually allows *the kick* to dominate the stroke, resulting in a much longer glide in the stretch position. A swimmer with a more powerful and often stockier, shorter upper body will wish to use his *arm action* to greater advantage. This usually means that there is very little glide in the stretch position because he allows his arms to take over from his legs almost before they have completed their kick.

While these variations may be perfectly suitable for the more able swimmer, anyone learning the stroke should be wary of deliberately copying them, or just falling into a similar habit. This applies especially to over-emphasis of the arms. It is very important to develop a reasonably good leg kick, and this you will be unable to do if you allow your arms to dominate. Gliding and kicking practice with your arms outstretched in front, thumbs together, is the best remedy for this fault.

BREAST STROKE RULES IN COMPETITIONS

In competitive events part of the swimmer's head must be above the water at all times in breast stroke. Additionally the following main rules have to be obeyed:

1. The swimmer's body must remain perfectly on the front. This means that you may not allow one shoulder to dip down lower than the other.
2. The leg kick must be simultaneous. This means that both feet must perform the action in perfect time.
3. The action of the feet must be symmetrical. This means that the screw kick version, where one foot is extended and the other foot shortened during the kick is not allowed.

In competitive races 'stroke judges' check that all the swimmers follow these rules and disqualify any offender. It is therefore very important to get rid of any of these faults right from the earliest stage if you have them. Even experienced swimmers can begin to swim with a faulty technique, so they too must concentrate on these points while training.

butterfly action

1. *Entry point:* the legs are about to kick and the head is well down between the arms as they enter the water.

2. *Start of pull:* elbows should be held high, hands pressing backwards against the water. Head is still down. Legs are straight out behind, causing little resistance.

3. *Mid-pull:* hands are kept close under the body as they pull. Head now starts to lift as breath continues to be exhaled.
   Legs are bending at the knees before the next kick.

4. *End of pull:* the head is now raised and the feet kick down again to keep the seat near the surface.

5. *Start of recovery:* the breath is taken in at this point. Note the raised elbows.
   The feet are now at their deepest point after the kick.

6. *Return to entry position:* hips are held high by dropping the head and kicking the feet as the arms swing over the surface ready for their next entry.

Dolphin butterfly

A good flat position for butterfly can be achieved by holding your breath for a complete arm cycle.

The dolphin butterfly stroke has been permitted in competitive swimming events for less than twenty years but now it is recognised as the most spectacular of the major racing strokes. It developed because swimmers wanted to swim the old-fashioned form of breast stroke faster. After pushing both arms vigorously through the water and past their shoulder line, the obvious thing to do to get more speed was to continue the movement and swing their arms clear of the water in the recovery phase. This became so popular that *butterfly* was born, a new stroke with a double vertical kicking action now known as the dolphin kick.

THE BASIC MOVEMENT

As the name suggests, the swimmer's body makes an undulating movement rather like a dolphin, and to begin with this is a good way of learning the basic technique:

Start with a push and glide from the side of the pool. Then, with thumbs together and hands stretched in front of your head, try to make a whipping action with your whole body, emphasising the final flick of your legs and feet. This can be done best while you are completely submerged, but it is also useful to try it on your back, and even lying on one side. You will soon be able to propel yourself across the width of the pool in this way. When you can, you are ready to learn the full and correct stroke.

BODY AND HEAD POSITION

Although the undulating movement in butterfly gives the impression of a great deal of up-and-down action, in fact this is a slightly false impression, and you should try hard to cut it down by keeping your seat and hips up near the surface right through the stroke.

Similarly, although you must lift your head to breathe, it should not be raised too high above the water, nor plunged too deeply below the surface. The swimmer should always feel that he is lifting his whole body *along* the surface of the water rather than up and over it.

THE LEG KICK

Although in some ways similar to the front crawl, the dolphin kick is slightly different. The feet and knees must remain *together* throughout the movement, which starts right up at the hips – or even higher, in the small of the back. The seat is lifted slightly and the legs begin their upwards phase with the knees kept straight until they are near the surface, when they bend. This is the start of the downward *whipping* action of the lower legs and feet which produces the thrust to drive your body forward. The ankles must be extended and the toes pointed as for the front crawl.

THE ARM ACTION

The very powerful action, performed by both arms at the same time, *is the main propelling force in butterfly,* and so great care must be taken to perform it correctly.

Entry. This is similar to the front crawl entry but is made with hands about twelve inches apart ahead of you (and never more than shoulder width apart). Your fingers should enter the water first, thumbs leading, followed by wrists and, last of all, by your elbows (which have been carefully lifted).

The pull. From this fully extended position your

There is a feeling of power as a butterfly swimmer surges forward (not upwards) over the water.

hands pull down and backwards. Before this, however, there is always a slight outwards movement of your hands and arms to about shoulder width. This gives you a stronger position from which to make the pull backwards and directly under your body. It is important to keep your elbows high during this first phase, or pressure on the water will be lost. When correctly done, the hands come almost together underneath your body before pushing back to the thighs. The shape formed by your hands during this phase closely resembles a keyhole, which is a useful image to keep in mind. If the final part of the pull is done quite fast, it can help lead into the *recovery.*

The recovery. This is a fast, low-swinging action of your arms over the water surface. The arms are kept fairly straight until they pass the line of your shoulders. Then your elbows bend and rise slightly to prepare for a good entry position.

BREATHING

The breathing action is very similar to breast stroke breathing. The breath has to be blown *out* into the water during the later part of the arm action, and taken *in* during the first part of the recovery phase.

Your mouth should be lifted just clear of the water surface, and care should be taken to make sure that your head is not thrown backwards too vigorously as this will thrust out your chin and chest to cause resistance.

In butterfly even more than in the other strokes it is vital to make a full exchange of air, and a really powerful blowing action is needed.

TIMING

This is the key to good butterfly swimming and requires a lot of practice before the stroke can be swum any distance without causing fatigue. There should be two leg kicks to each complete arm cycle, the first when your hands are stretched out in front just after entry, and the second at the end of the arm pull, just before the recovery. They are both necessary at that time to make sure that your hips stay near the surface.

A correct head movement is also important: lifted slightly when you breathe in, and dropped forward between your arms at the end of the recovery just before entry (as in the middle illustration opposite).

PRACTICES

Now try to master the leg kick proper:

1. Hold the rail or gutter, lift your seat, raise your legs and then kick down with the feet, toes pointed. Repeat this a number of times and try to keep your head and shoulders quite steady.

2. Try the same practice, holding a float (or board) in front of you. Experiment with head up and steady, and also with your face in the water.

3. Repeat this a number of times across the width of the pool, then try it on your back, float (or board) held to your chest. Then on one side, float (or board) held out in front in one hand, keeping the other hand at your side. Try not to wriggle too much but make your feet and legs do the work.

4. Standing, practise the arm action, first simply as 'pull and throw', and later with the correct path of movement: the keyhole pull. Progress to walking along the pool, pulling yourself forward with your arms.

5. Push and glide. Kick three times with arms in front, then pull and throw. Repeat this across the width of the pool.

6. Experiment with only two kicks, trying to fit them in correctly, one at the beginning of the pull and one at the end.

7. Try variations of breathing, including holding your breath for a few strokes, breathing only every second stroke and once every stroke cycle.

8. Practise pulling, holding a float between your legs.

Butterfly recovery

Your arms should both come forward at exactly the same time during the recovery, little fingers uppermost. Keep them well clear of the water. Anyone with shoulders as flexible as this swimmer will have a big advantage in performing the butterfly recovery.

Butterfly entry

Raised elbows and a slightly dropped position for fingers and thumbs bring your hands into a good entry position. Your chin should be tucked in and your face dropped into the water.

Butterfly pull

The bent arm pull drives the body forward. This is the main propelling force in butterfly and should be continued as far as the thighs before beginning the recovery. At this point your head is just coming up to breathe.

A swimmer who can perform the four racing strokes reasonably well will soon want to put them to the test either by racing against other swimmers or by seeing how fast he can swim over a set distance such as a width or a length of the pool.

Because the start for front crawl, breast stroke and butterfly is done from the side of the pool – often from a raised starting block that enables the swimmer to dive further out over the pool before actually entering the water – it is important to be able to perform a good starting dive. This will get you off efficiently and help you to move into your swimming stroke quickly and smoothly. A bad start, on the other hand, will not only lose you valuable time and distance but will also almost certainly cause you to swim the first few strokes badly as you will be in the wrong position.

The racing dive is easier to understand (and perform) if you break it down into four stages: *stance, take-off, entry* and *the start of the swimming stroke.*

THE STANCE

The stance is the position of readiness you adopt in a race when the starter gives the command 'Take your marks'. Correct positioning of your feet, knees, trunk, head and hands is very important.

Feet: should point straight forward and be comfortably apart (about four inches) to give you good balance. Toes should be curled round the edge of the block or poolside for a firm grip.

Knees: a very slight bend is all that is needed. But make sure that your knees are directly in line over your feet and not turned outwards.

Trunk: again only a slight bend forward at the hips is needed, allowing your back to curve naturally. Avoid bending too far forward as this causes tension of your stomach and chest muscles and restricts your breathing.

Head: you should look into the water straight ahead and just a few feet in front of you. If you look further down the pool you will be forced to raise your head, which will tighten your throat muscles, again restricting your breathing.

Hands: these can be held out below and in front of your knees, or else behind your back as shown in the illustration.

You are now ready for the second stage: *the take-off.*

THE TAKE-OFF

When the starting signal is given you must explode

The racing start: for front crawl, breast stroke and butterfly

into immediate action. Your body should topple forward and, precisely at the moment of overbalance, you must be ready to drive hard with your legs away from the block or side. At the same time swing your arms vigorously forwards and upwards, hands joined with locked thumbs above your head. The combined movement of your arm swing and leg thrust will take you into a long streamlined position and, if this second stage is performed correctly, you will be in the right position for *the entry.*

THE ENTRY

The angle at which you enter the water is important. You must be able to feel yourself cutting into the water like an arrow, not flopping on top of it. Many swimmers try to dive too far out into the pool, with the result that they come down on top of the water with a lot of noise and splash and little forward movement. A 'flat' entry can be a painful experience as well as having a braking effect as you enter the water. It is better to aim shorter with a really strong take-off drive and a good stretch position.

THE START OF THE SWIMMING STROKE

The last stage of the racing dive occurs when you are actually in the water and about to start swimming. The best moment to begin making your first stroke movements is the moment when the forward speed of your entry is the speed you can swim at. If you make your first stroke too soon, you will interrupt the fast speed of your dive. If you make it too late, you will lose your speed and have to build it up again.

Experiment until you find the moment that is right for you.

FRONT CRAWL AND BUTTERFLY STARTS

In these two strokes try to get your legs moving first, just before starting your first arm pull. And in front crawl starts, a few strokes made while holding your breath will help you to get moving smoothly.

BREAST STROKE START

This is a shade more complicated because in competitive swimming you are allowed to make one (but only one) complete stroke movement (that is, *one arm pull and recovery,* and *one leg kick*) before coming to the surface to start your second stroke cycle. This is of more advantage to older and stronger swimmers: most young swimmers do best to concentrate on perfecting a really good dive.

3

2

4

Turns: for front crawl, breast stroke and butterfly

Turns are as important as starts to the competitive swimmer, yet a good swim ruined by a bad turn is very common – even more common than a good swim spoiled by a poor start.

The turn must be not regarded as an opportunity for easing up, but rather as a change of direction that you have to make as quickly and correctly as possible. The ways in which the various turns must be performed in competitive events are clearly laid down in the rules controlling front crawl freestyle, breast stroke and butterfly races. Some of the requirements differ but certain basic techniques apply equally to all three:

THE APPROACH

Whatever the stroke, the approach must be made *at full speed,* without any slackening off in preparation for the turn. In fact, the swimmer should take a very positive attitude and 'attack' the turn. This applies especially in butterfly, so that the swimmer reaches the wall at exactly the right point in the stroke, that is, when the arms are at the end of a recovery action.

THE TURNING MOVEMENT

This must be done as fast as possible but without too much tension.

THE PUSH-OFF

Like the push-off in starts from the side, this is in many ways the most important part of the turn because the swimmer's position at this point will affect the way the first few strokes are swum *after* the turn.

The body must be fully extended in a streamlined position, head in line, hands together, knees and ankles stretched. The push is more effective if the swimmer's body is completely submerged. It should not be started until feet and hands are in the correct position.

A turn that is done carelessly can cost the race.

BREAST STROKE AND BUTTERFLY TURNS

The rules controlling breast stroke and butterfly turns are almost the same. Unlike freestyle turns, in which only the swimmer's feet have to touch the side, *the touch in breast stroke and butterfly must be made with both hands, at the same time and at the same level.* (The breast stroke rules also allow one complete stroke cycle to be performed underwater after the turn.)

At the touch the swimmer must be looking straight forward and up and out of the water. The shoulders then take over the lead, twisting vigorously to whichever side the swimmer prefers. At the same time the legs are pulled up underneath, while a sort of swivelling movement between the shoulders and the seat takes the shoulders away from the wall and down into the water. This also brings the feet, legs and hips up near the surface and close to the wall. Thus the swimmer's body is again flat and horizontal and his head just under the surface ready for the push-off.

The swivelling action needs a lot of practice and care must be taken to place the feet correctly on the wall, neither too high nor too low, so that at push-off the body is driven straight off the wall. Some swimmers start the push-off slightly on one side, but the laws demand that *by the time the swimmer's feet leave the wall, his body should be perfectly on the front.*

breast stroke and butterfly turn

1. *Approach:* this must be at full speed, driving hard to the wall.

2. *Touch:* both hands must touch at the same time and at the same level.

3. *Turn:* a powerful swivel of shoulders and legs helps the swimmer round.

4. *Push-off:* a key position. Feet firmly against the wall, knees bent, and the head and upper body dropping into line.

5. *The glide:* everything in line, just below the surface after a powerful push off the wall.

1

5

tumble turn

Three phases in the tumble turn: 1. The forward somersault. 2. The twist mid-way through the somersault. 3. The end of the tumble with head between arms, hands in front, and feet ready to stretch back to make the strong thrust off the wall.

1

2

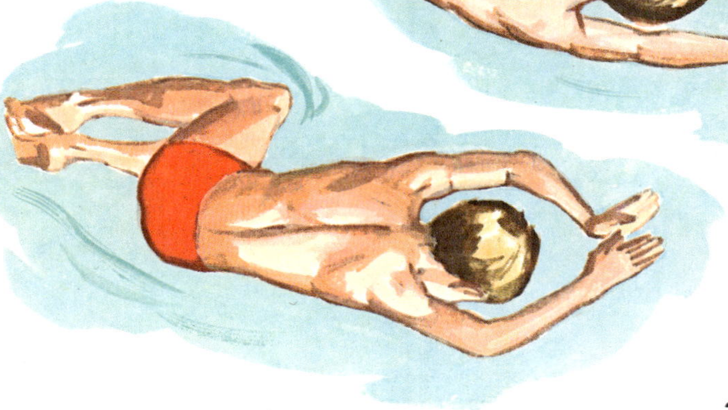

3

THE FRONT CRAWL TURN

The rules permit the front crawl turn to be made without the swimmer's hands touching the side of the pool at all as long as his *feet* do so. This allows the use of the fast *tumble turn,* sometimes called the *somersault turn,* or *flip turn.*

THE TUMBLE TURN

The most difficult part of this turn is deciding exactly how far away from the wall to begin it. The distance varies for each person and depends on the speed of the approach and the length of the swimmer's legs. Lots of experimenting has to be done until each swimmer knows automatically the correct spot at which he must begin his turn.

The tumble turn is really a combination of a forward somersault and a half twist. At the right point for starting the turn, begin by pushing your head down under the surface, tuck your body and legs up under you and somersault forwards. Halfway over, one shoulder drops and twists, and your feet and legs reach out towards the wall for the push-off. At the same time your lower hand presses on the water to help to complete the movement and get your body back on the front again.

PRACTISING THE TUMBLE TURN

The best way to learn the tumble turn is to practise the forward somersault action first, on its own and away from the wall. When you can do it reasonably well, practise it close to the wall. The twist can then be added at the end of the somersault and gradually brought forward until the two are combined.

1

2

Starts and turns for back crawl

The same general advice given on pages 34–37 for front starts and turns, applies also to these.

BACK CRAWL START

The stance. The starting dive is done with the swimmer already in the water, facing the pool wall and with his back to the racing course.

Hands. These hold the starting blocks, rail or gutter, whichever is available. They should be about shoulder width apart.

Feet. These are placed against the wall, toes below the surface, a few inches apart and preferably with one foot slightly higher than the other to provide an alternative push in case one foot slips – and this can happen quite easily on a tiled wall.

Body. The rest of the body sits comfortably in a curled position with the arms straight and eyes looking directly ahead at the wall. On the command 'Take your marks' the swimmer's arms bend, bringing the body up and out of the water and the head forward towards the rail. This is the position of readiness and is held until the starting signal is given.

THE TAKE-OFF

On the starting signal the swimmer must thrust up and away from the wall with the legs, out and over the water, at the same time arching the back and swinging the arms back over the head into a fully extended position (as shown in the illustration). The head should be kept in line with the body and not held up or dropped too far back. The head position is very important in the back stroke and a great deal of practice has to be done to produce the best possible position.

ENTRY

This needs a lot of experiment but if the correct position is achieved in the air, with the body fully stretched, the entry will almost certainly be good. Remember that on entry the water will go up into your nose unless you learn to blow out vigorously once your head goes under.

3

back crawl start

1. *Stance:* relaxed but concentrating, with hands and feet in the correct position. Feet must be below the water line.
2. *Take your marks!* With a pull on the hands, head and shoulders are drawn closer to the wall.
3. *Take-off:* hands swing up and back, and at the same time your legs drive hard off the wall, lifting your body up and back out of the water.
4. *The stretch and entry:* the back should arch nicely, the head should drop back towards the water and the arms should be fully stretched beyond your head to make a smooth entry.

4

Since both hands are above the swimmer's head after a back crawl start, it is a fairly simple matter to leave one hand where it is and start pulling with the other. When this hand reaches your side, start your normal stroke cycle. Most swimmers begin their leg kick just before starting the arm pull.

THE BACK CRAWL TURN

Although this turn is technically the most difficult to do, all backstrokers seem able to produce a better turn than swimmers of the other racing strokes. This is probably because backstrokers cannot see the wall they are approaching and, having no wish to bump their heads or hurt their fingers, develop a better technique out of sheer self preservation.

In back crawl races there should always be a line of flags across the pool about five metres from the wall. These are to help the swimmers to judge when to make their turns without having to keep turning round to look at the wall.

On the approach the feet must kick hard right up to the moment the leading hand touches the wall, palm flat and fingers pointing down to the bottom of the pool (about a foot below the surface). The head and shoulders follow the hand back under the water, the knees bend and the curled up body is lifted over the surface, pivoting round the shoulders. After this twist, the feet are brought down vigorously against the wall at about the same point where the hands first touched. The tucked up body is now under the surface, hands above the head and ready for the powerful thrust off the wall. As in starts, the body should be in the straight, streamlined position after the thrust. The feet begin their kick and the stroke cycle begins as described for the start.

PRACTISING THE BACK CRAWL TURN

When practising the turn, start from the push-off. Get this right first, then add the twisting part, and finally the approach to the wall. Practise using both left and right hand to make the touch so that you can turn equally well whichever hand comes to the wall.

back crawl turn

1. *The touch:* this is made while still on your back, with your hand flat on the wall and fingers pointing down.

2. *The turn:* head and shoulders drop and spin, bringing your legs over the top.

3. *The push-off:* with the feet ready to push off the wall, your body and head are perfectly positioned, with hands stretched beyond your head, your fingers streamlined and together.

Relay racing

1 2

For many competitors the most enjoyable races are the team relays. Certainly they are the most exciting events for the spectators, especially if they are closely contested races with the lead constantly changing right to the finish. In theory the team with the four fastest swimmers *should* win, but so much can be lost or gained during the take-overs that quite often a slightly slower team with good take-overs can beat another four who are individually faster swimmers.

FREESTYLE AND MEDLEY RELAYS

There are two main types of relay: *freestyle relays,* in which the swimmers may perform any stroke they choose (almost always the front crawl as this is the fastest stroke), and *medley relays,* in which each of the four swimmers in the team must swim *one* of the racing strokes *in the following order:*

1. Backstroke (starting in the water).
2. Breast stroke (starting from a dive).
3. Butterfly (starting from a dive).
4. Freestyle (usually front crawl and starting from a dive).

THE TAKE-OVER

Learning to perfect a well-timed take-over technique is as important for a swimmer as it is for a runner. The take-over rule states that the outgoing swimmer must still be in contact with the side or the starting block when the incoming swimmer touches the end of the pool. The important words here are 'in contact with'. This does not mean being perfectly still and the ideal position for the outgoing swimmer would be for him to be fully stretched out into his dive with only his toes touching the side or block at the precise moment of the touch. Unfortunately when a swimmer attempts to do this, there is, first of all, the danger of an error in his timing. Secondly, there is the danger that to the judge's eye such a take-over always *appears* to be an illegal take-off. It is therefore necessary for the outgoing swimmer to play a little bit safer and make sure of an *obviously* legal take-over. On the other hand valuable time can be lost if the outgoing swimmer 'dallies' too long on the block after the touch. The best timing can be achieved only through regular practice with team mates and some experimenting. A coach or helper is also needed to watch from the side and feed back information on whether the take-over was too early, too late or just right.

THE RELAY SWIMMER'S RESPONSIBILITIES

Each swimmer in a relay team has responsibilities:

The incoming swimmer must maintain his swimming speed at full stretch. To slow down will ruin the take-over because once the outgoing swimmer has started his dive he is fully committed and cannot regain his balance.

The outgoing swimmer must watch his team mate from some distance out, gauging the speed of his

3

1. *A well-timed take over:* the outgoing swimmer has reached the point of overbalance and is ready to drive off the block just as his team mate touches the wall.

2. *An illegal take-over:* the outgoing swimmer will have left the block before the incoming swimmer has touched the wall.

3. *A late take-over:* the incoming swimmer has already touched the wall and had time to lift his head before the outgoing swimmer has started his dive.

approach and preparing for his own dive. He should watch the incoming swimmer's head or a point around his waist as these will move about less than his arms and legs. At the right moment the outgoing swimmer must launch powerfully out into his dive, keeping right in the centre of the lane.

Since we know that the shortest distance between two points is a straight line, it is important that the whole team should swim right up and down the centre of the lane throughout the race. This is fairly simple where there are raised starting blocks and there is no danger of the outgoing swimmer hitting his incoming team mate's feet. However, the danger does exist, or at least it will often *appear* to do so to many swimmers, especially those who may not have a powerful starting dive. In these cases, the outgoing swimmer may stand slightly to one side for the take-over but should dive and surface in such a way that he immediately starts swimming in the centre of the lane.

DECIDING THE TEAM'S SWIMMING ORDER

In freestyle relays the swimming order of the team will be determined by a number of things:

An inexperienced swimmer, or one with a previously poor take-over record, will swim first.

The known strengths and weaknesses of the opponents may decide the point at which a team places its own strongest and weakest members.

For example, if it is known that a particular opponent will only swim as fast as is necessary to beat the person next to him, it is often advisable to put in the team's slowest member against him.

The individual preference of the team members is also taken into account, although normal practice is to put the fastest swimmer on the final 'anchor' leg since he is the best man to fight off a challenge or to make one.

On the other hand, a coach will often reverse this order completely to try to bring out the best in his team by giving them a good lead right from the start.

The order may also be influenced if any of the team has competed in earlier races. The longer the rest between events the better, so any swimmer who has just swum an individual event may be put near the end of the relay order.

A training session in full swing. The swimmers go round the lanes in circles, working at their stroke practices.

Training practices and racing hints

Once you can swim the four racing strokes, or at least a couple of them and can manage the right starts and turns, it is time to improve your performance still further. But this can be done only if you are prepared to follow a regular system of training, planned to improve your fitness and the five S's: skill, speed, strength, stamina and suppleness.

Distance swims, sectional practices, interval or repetition swims, sprints and stroke drills are the normal routines found in a swimmer's training schedule. They can be combined in various ways to suit the needs of the most modest performer or the advanced skills of an Olympic champion.

DISTANCE SWIMS
Your fitness can be measured by your ability to keep up a reasonably good stroke over a long distance. It is pointless swimming on and on if your stroke technique has broken down, as by then it will be hopelessly inefficient. However, by starting on shortish distances at a fairly gentle pace and breathing properly and regularly in each stroke cycle, you can build up the distance over which you can maintain a good stroke. Once you can swim 400 metres or so then there is really no limit to the distance you can progressively undertake.

SECTIONAL PRACTICES
These practices break the strokes down into *kicking* and *pulling* and are usually done holding a float (or kick board) – in your hands for kicking practice, and between your legs for pulling practice. Both can be done over any distance you choose but are best if you work at a good hard, fast pace.

INTERVAL OR REPETITION SWIMS
A chosen distance, usually 50 or 100 metres, is repeated a number of times with a rest between efforts, that is after each chosen 'length'. The rest can be short or long, depending on how fast you intend to swim and on how hard you wish to work your muscles, or heart and lungs. For example, you can swim 8 × 50 metres with ten seconds rest after each, or 4 × 100 metres with one or two minutes rest between repetitions.

The aim when doing these swims should be to keep each effort around the same time. They will vary a bit of course, but if you find that you are unable to keep a fairly even pace throughout, then you have possibly started too quickly on the earlier ones. It is better to give yourself a target which you can reach fairly easily at first, then gradually get faster when you find this target becomes too easy.

SPRINTS
As the term suggests, these are efforts swum at or near flat-out speed and test the swimmer to the full. The distance for sprint practices is usually kept fairly short, 25 or 50 metres, and a fairly longish rest is usually needed between sprints. There is always the danger here that the swimmer will be tempted to use sheer brute force to achieve good times, sacrificing stroke control in the process. This ruins the whole object of the practice and should be avoided. A fast-revving action must be your main aim but not at the expense of the stroke: good stroke control must be kept at the same time.

STROKE DRILLS
Here the strokes are again broken down so that you can concentrate your practice on any particular part of the stroke in which you have a weakness. The parts can be practised in various ways. For example:

Front crawl: one arm pulling at a time, the other held at the side or out in front. Swimming with your head up, looking at the point of entry of the hand.

Back crawl: single arm and double arm pulling. The crawl arm drills help to teach the correct path of

movement for the hands and arms, stressing particularly the last phase of the pull.

Dolphin butterfly: dolphin kick underwater on the back and side. This drill helps to develop the dolphin-like undulation of the body.

Breast stroke: kicking with (*a*) thumbs locked in front to stress the importance of holding the stretch position, (*b*) arms held at sides, trying to touch the hands with the heels, thus making sure that the feet are well pulled up, and (*c*) on the back with hands over head, keeping knees down under the surface, thus getting the knees and thighs in the best position. *Breast stroke: pulling,* with a crawl or dolphin kick.

These and similar drills can be used to develop a good 'feel' of the water and general watermanship.

TRAINING SCHEDULES

From the practices described above you can make up a training programme to suit your own needs and your own particular weaknesses. The important thing is that whatever your programme is, *everything must be done correctly,* and you must gradually increase it so that you are setting yourself a higher and higher target.

Here are two sample schedules based on 1500 metres and 3000 metres.

SAMPLE SCHEDULE: 3000 METRES

1. Swim 400 metres – 100 metres in each stroke, alternate length fast and slow.
2. Kick 6 × 50 metres – 10 seconds rest – repeat same time.
3. Pull 8 × 50 metres in front crawl – 15 seconds rest.
4. Swim 2 × 200 metres – 1 minute rest – repeat time.
5. Swim 4 × 100 metres – 1 minute rest – repeat time (faster than half the time taken for the 200 metres).
6. Swim 400 metres in your second choice stroke – alternate lengths easy and hard.
7. 6 × 50 metres – sprints – as much rest as needed.
8. 8 × 25 metres – sprints – 1 minute rest.
9. Swim 200 metres easy – loosen off.

SAMPLE SCHEDULE: 1500 METRES

1. Swim 200 metres – easy, vary the strokes, loosen off.
2. Kick 200 metres – one length easy, one length hard.
3. Pull 300 metres in front crawl.
4. Swim 3 × 50 metres with 30 seconds rest after each one.
5. Swim 200 metres in your second choice stroke.
6. Sprint 8 × 25 metres with 1 minute rest between.

RACING HINTS

Whether you are a beginner or a fairly seasoned competitor it is important to make sure that when you actually come to a race you are able to give of your best. All the hard training you have done can go for nothing if you make a silly mistake just before the race. The following points should help to steer you clear of some of the errors frequently made:

1. Check in advance the starting time of the meet, and if possible at what point in the programme your event will take place.

2. Arrive in plenty of time to have a warm-up before the start and remember to report to the steward. A useful warm-up schedule is given below.

3. Always take as many swimming costumes as you will need for the warm-up and *all* your races, including heats and finals.

4. Other necessary equipment includes a track suit or some similar warm clothing for wearing between events, warm socks and sneakers. Take an adequate supply of large towels. No swimmer is comfortable drying off with an already wet towel.

5. After your warm-up change into a dry costume and track suit. Find a comfortable, dry place to sit and wait for your race. Don't waste your energy and the chance of a good swim by running about and fooling around. On the other hand, don't let your muscles get too stiff; stand up and have a good stretch now and again.

6. Think *positively* about your race and how you intend to swim it. Convince *yourself* that you will swim faster than ever before.

7. Listen to the starter as he gives his commands in earlier races. This will help you get used to his orders and help to avoid the most wasteful mistake a swimmer can make: a false start.

8. After your race, whether you won or lost, talk to your opponents, congratulating them if they won, or consoling them if they lost. And if you won, be happy but humble. If you lost, be determined to do better next time, but try to be dignified and keep control of your emotions.

If you follow this advice you will enjoy competitive swimming, win or lose.

PRE-RACE WARM-UP SCHEDULE

1. Swim until feeling loose, e.g. 200–300 metres.
2. Kick a few 50-metre lengths, e.g. 4 × 50 metres.
3. Pull some 50-metre lengths, e.g. 4 × 50 metres – increase speed.
4. Swim a few lengths at race pace, e.g. 2 × 50 metres.
5. Practise turns at both ends of the pool.
6. Practise starts from the blocks.
7. Swim a few sprints, e.g. 4 × 25 metres.
8. Loosen off swim, e.g. 200 metres easy.

Diving practices in the water

To return to the surface after a deep push and glide, turn your head and hands upwards.

Diving is the most exciting part of a swim for many people, and lots of swimmers happily spend more time diving into and climbing out of the water than they spend actually swimming around in it.

Diving has its own special techniques and to avoid any uncomfortable experiences it is best to build up your skills from simple diving exercises in the water to the more complex dives made from the boards. Even though you may already be able to enter the water head first from the side of the pool, the practices described in the following pages will form a solid basis for a good diving style and for more advanced dives later.

The first and most important thing is to be perfectly happy about putting your face and head right under the water, and opening your eyes under the surface.

Try picking things up from the bottom of the pool, starting with largish objects that are easy to see and handle, and then progress to coins and other small objects which are more difficult to spot and pick up. As you pick them up try to get your head and face as close to the bottom of the pool as you can. Next move to a slightly deeper part of the pool so that you have to jump off the bottom before you can get your head down. Then advance to jumping from one of the lower steps or towards the corner rail or gutter. Work with a partner and see who can pick up most objects in a given time.

PUSH AND GLIDE

The push and glide practice already described on page 11 is a very valuable preparation for diving. The important thing is to keep your head absolutely steady between your arms, and your face completely in the water. Now is the time to check again that you still have a long, fully stretched position with all joints (fingers, elbows, shoulders, hips, knees and ankles) fully extended.

Once you can push and glide smoothly along a fair distance on or just below the surface, try aiming for the bottom of the pool, making sure that your forefingers are touching, thumbs linked and palms facing downwards. Your hands must *never* be held palm to palm as this will cause you to cut too sharply through the water, something that will be dangerous later on when you are entering from a height.

Then try to glide back to the surface from the bottom of the pool by pointing your wrists and hands upwards. When you feel that you can do this, go on to glide down and through a partner's legs. This tests whether you have good control over the direction of your dive.

Now you are ready to start making steeper dives. Sit on one of the lower steps of the pool and push and glide downwards to the bottom. Repeat this from successively higher steps until you are pushing and gliding from the top step, where your feet will be just above the waterline as you push off. Concentrate still on getting a good stretch position to your whole body and – most important of all – keep your head steady between your arms.

A later practice, leading to the plain header, is to stand on the pool bottom, jump up with hands and arms stretched above your head, bend your knees and bend slightly forward at the hips. This will cause you to spring out of the water, up and over the surface, and then to come down again, head first, rather like a dolphin. Try this over a line on the pool bottom or over your partner's outstretched arms to encourage a forward movement.

Handstanding on the pool bottom is another good preliminary to diving proper. To begin with, this is best done by curling into a ball, head under the surface, eyes open, and then reaching down with your hands to the bottom. When you can do this easily and return to your feet with equal ease, try stretching your legs and feet up above you. At first, you may well topple over, but by bending in the middle or even tucking up into a ball again, you will return to a normal standing position immediately. This will be very useful practice for later stages of diving when you may have to try to correct an overbalanced entry position.

When you can manage this, concentrate on getting a good stretched and straight body, with knees and ankles held firm. Your toes, of course, will point upwards. Now try this from a standing position in water about chest height. With your arms stretched above your head, hands apart, bend your knees and lean forward a little more than for the similar practice described above. In fact, to begin with the upper part of your body may be almost horizontal at the surface of the water. When you spring upwards let your head and arms go down to the bottom, and try to hold your handstand perfectly still for a few seconds.

You can also spend time usefully in the water trying various rolls and somersaults which will help your diving later on. Again these can be started as you lie in the water and gradually developed until you can perform them jumping off the pool bottom.

Handstanding on the pool bottom and diving down through a partner's legs are useful practices for getting your head well down below the surface.

Dives from the poolside

From diving practices in the water the next logical step is diving from the poolside, and the same firm head position and good body stretch is needed.

For obvious reasons the dives described in this and the following sections should only be made into water of adequate depth. The right depth for the dives in this section depends on the height of the diver, but certainly more than three feet of water is needed and probably nearer five feet for absolute safety.

SITTING DIVE
Sit as close to the edge of the pool as you can and place your feet on the rail, gutter or ledge, whichever you find is most comfortable. With your knees apart, stretch your arms downwards, almost between your knees. Link your hands with locked thumbs and palms facing downwards. Keep your head well down and your chin on your chest. Now topple forward until you overbalance. At this point give a push with your feet against the rail or channel and start to straighten your knees. Aim to move slightly forward and out over the water rather than letting yourself tumble straight down into it.

Whatever happens, *keep your head down between your arms* to avoid an unpleasant 'flop' on the water. After entry let your movement through the water continue as far as the drive of the dive takes you until you come to a natural stop.

KNEELING DIVE
This is similar to the sitting dive but is made from a slightly higher position without actually standing. One knee is placed right at the edge of the pool, with the other foot alongside it but a couple of inches away to give a good firm base. Hold your head and hands as in the sitting dive but with your back a little less rounded, allowing your hands to aim further out from the side. The chin-on-chest and head-between-arms position is even more important now that you are going to dive from a higher point and will therefore meet the water with greater impact.

THE CROUCH DIVE
As the name suggests, this is done from a crouched position at the edge of the pool. Grip the edge with your toes for support. Bend your knees fully and raise your arms over your head, pointing down towards the water. As you topple forward and overbalance, give a forceful push with your feet, straightening your knees as you do so. This will drive you down into the water

The modified header: piked (*left*), less sharply piked (*middle*), and almost upright (*right*).

in line after your hands. Again, on entry hold the stretch position and, by turning your hands up after entry, avoid going too far below the surface.

Don't try to dive too deep, but aim out a little way down the pool.

As your confidence increases the crouch position can gradually become more upright.

THE LUNGE DIVE

Place one foot behind the other on the poolside, the front leg well bent and the rear leg straighter. Raise your arms above your head in line with your body, head down and chin in. As you overbalance, push off with your front leg and bring your feet together in the air. Again your line of entry into the water should be outwards, away from the side. This dive leads quite easily and naturally to the modified header.

THE MODIFIED HEADER

The final practice from the side is a modified version of the plain header itself, and is done from a piked position, that is, with your body bent forward at the hips. Hold your hands and arms in a 'Y' position beyond your head, palms facing forward. Bend your knees and then straighten them to thrust you away from the side. The top half of your body will then be directed downwards towards the water.

As your execution of this dive improves and your confidence grows, gradually aim to make your entry closer to the side, using the lines marked on the bottom to guide you. And gradually reduce the amount of 'piking' at the hips until you are taking off from an almost straight position.

THE PLUNGE DIVE

This is really the same as the racing start described on page 34 except that when it is performed on its own the emphasis is on achieving a long gliding position and not on sheer speed into the stroke. The angle of entry will usually be shallower when used as a racing start.

If you want to perform the plunge dive well:

1. Start from a well balanced position, feet apart and flat on the poolside.
2. Make sure of a good thrust forward with your legs.
3. Swing your arms forward at the right time (just as your legs straighten) and bring your hands together with your arms symmetrical, close to your head.
4. Keep your head down and cut into the water. Don't slap the surface with your hands and forearms.
5. After entry hold the stretched position with thumbs locked until your speed is well down.

This is the very basic dive you must perfect if you wish to progress to more advanced diving. It can be done from the poolside or from higher as long as the water is deep enough (at least deeper than the diver's full stretch height when his arms are held above his head).

STANCE
Stance in the header is a very erect position: feet together, knees straight, body in perfect line. The arms are raised overhead with hands just wider than shoulder width apart. Palms face forward, and thumbs and fingers are together. Keep your head in line between your arms and look straight ahead.

TAKE-OFF
Bend your knees straight forward, transferring your body weight over the balls of your feet. Then straighten your knees vigorously and stretch your ankles and feet as hard as you can. As long as your thrust is directed straight up through your hips, the dive will be well executed. Avoid the common tendency to drop your arms down at this stage.

FLIGHT
This should follow the path of a perfect curve if you have done everything correctly. After the slight bending of the hips which takes place at take-off your body should straighten out just before entry. Your hands also come together then for the entry.

ENTRY
If the water is deep enough your aim should be to make a *vertical* entry. This, however, takes time and practice to achieve. Think of your fingers making a 'hole' in the water and your head and the rest of your body following them through the hole. Don't lift your head back, as the top of it should be first through the hole after your hands.

For a really good-looking entry the whole body should be stretched and pointed from finger tips to toes. The dive is not completed until your *whole body* is in the water, and you should follow through right to the bottom of the pool.

COMMON FAULTS
Although a simple dive, the plain header is often

The plain header

The main features of the plain header are: 1. The upright stance. 2. The drive up through the hips. 3. The bend at the hips. 4. The gradual straightening of the body in flight. 5. The fully stretched position at entry, which should be as near vertical as possible.

performed badly because the diver fails to guard against one or other of the common faults listed here:

Stance: failing to take up a controlled position, especially poking the head and chin forward, or allowing the stomach to stick out. *Remedy:* try to feel as *long and thin* as possible. Practise the position in a mirror to get the right feeling.

Take-off: failing to drive far enough *upwards*. This will cause a very shallow dive and can best be corrected by fixing your gaze slightly above head level. *Remedy:* at the moment you push with your legs, try to imagine that you are being lifted up by your chest.

Flight: lack of control in head, arms and feet. *Remedy:* once you have left the poolside there is nothing you can do about your actual flight path, as this is decided by the angle of thrust at the take-off. So the secret is to make sure that your take-off is correct.

Entry: again sloppiness in hands and feet are the commonest faults. *Remedy:* correct by concentrating on *feeling* your fingers and ankles are together and stretched.

Basic diving positions

straight

There are three basic diving positions in which dives can be performed: straight, tuck and pike. The many variant dives seen in competitive diving events will all be performed in one of these positions.

STRAIGHT DIVES
This is the position described for the plain header (*page 48*). The diver's legs and body are perfectly straight, and the feet are together with toes pointed. The stomach is flat and the arms held straight above the head. In some straight dives the back may be arched.

PIKED DIVES
In the pike position the body is bent at the hips, and that is the only part of the body that is out of line. The position can be performed *closed* (with the diver's arms coming right down to touch his toes or holding behind his calves) or *open* (arms held level with the diver's shoulders).

TUCK DIVES
In the tuck position the whole body is curled up as small and compactly as possible. In order to hold this fairly difficult position the diver's hands wrap round his legs just below his knees and hold his thighs and knees against his chest. Elbows must be kept tucked in too.

You can perform all three positions from the poolside but it is best to try them as *feet-first* jumps before trying a head-first entry into the water. Aim for a good 'entry' position in your practice jumps: as vertical as possible with hands held down by your sides, feet and legs together, with toes pointed downwards.

Now try them as actual dives from the poolside. The take-off is similar to that for the header but aim to get as high as possible in the flight phase to give yourself a better chance of getting into the various positions.

Twists and somersaults are a more advanced form of diving. To perform them properly as part of a competitive diving programme you need the instruction of a coach, and it is beyond the scope of this book to deal with them. However, you can get a lot of fun just from trying twists from the side, or somersaults from a crouch position into the water.

WORKING FROM THE BOARDS
Once you have had a sound early training in the key dives and preliminary practices, you can begin to perform the dives from the diving boards, working to perfect the different phases making up the dive. Pay special attention to the following points:

Starting position. For running dives the starting position is the first step of the diver's run, whereas in standing dives it is the moment when the diver is stationary on the end of the board, body erect and arms at his sides. Although the actual approach to these starting positions is not judged, divers should always make it as smooth and controlled an approach as possible. This may just influence the judge's overall assessment of the dive, and also helps to make sure that the diver is properly prepared to execute his dive with a more positive, *thinking* attitude. There should be at least four steps in a running dive, and

tuck

pike

The straight position: there is no bend at the hips or knees in this graceful and well-controlled dive.

The piked position: this is a *closed* pike position with hands close to the diver's feet. Knees and ankles must be kept perfectly straight.

The tuck position: the body is pulled into this curled up position, which is held before the diver straightens out for entry.

any fewer than this will automatically bring a reduction in your marks.

Take-off. The diver takes off from both feet on the springboard, and from one or both feet on the fixed board. The take-off must be performed in a bold, and confident fashion, achieving a good height in doing so. As already explained in previous chapters, it is the direction and amount of thrust at the take-off which will play a major part in deciding how good most dives ultimately become.

Flight. Once in the air, off the board, the diver's body must pass through or be held in one of the three positions illustrated and described here. Whichever of these is chosen, it must be held as long as necessary, and shown very clearly. The arms may be held in any position that suits the diver, but they should not get in the way and must be under control throughout the dive.

One of the most important points to note is that the diver's toes must be fully stretched and well pointed to give a long, graceful appearance. The feet and legs must also be kept together.

Entry. The main aim here is to achieve as vertical a position on entry as possible. 'Going over' beyond the vertical or – slightly less frequent – failing to achieve the vertical position will certainly result in the judges deducting marks. In fact, this is usually the most heavily penalised fault in diving.

In the normal, head-first entry, the arms should be held above the head, kept straight at the elbows and with the hands as close together as possible.

Once the diver actually disappears under the surface the dive is regarded as completed, and so the return to the surface is not marked at all.

forward dive
back dive
inward dive
reverse dive

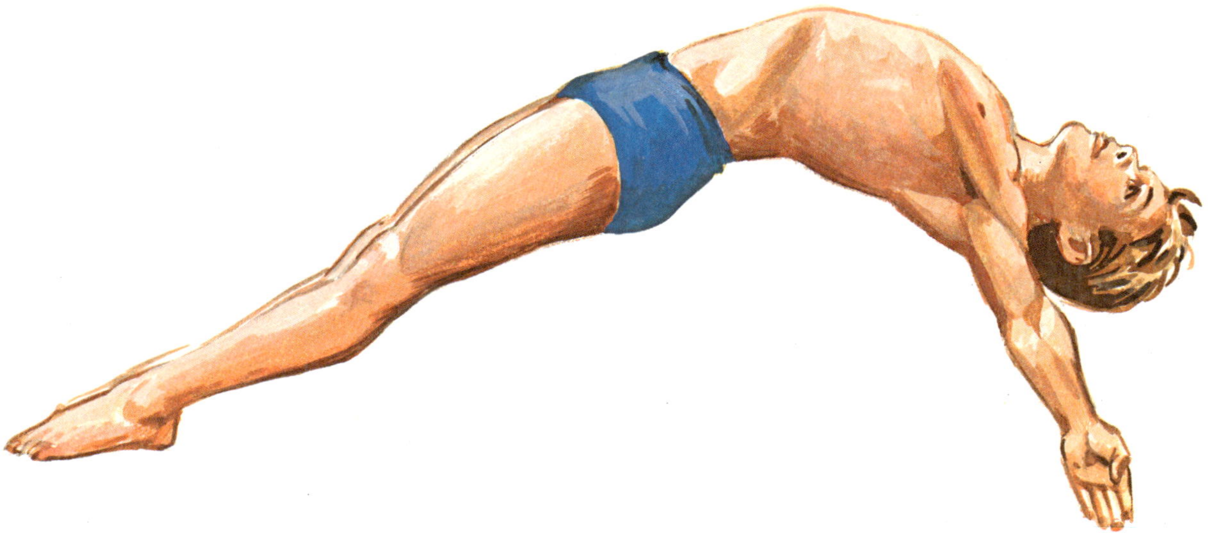

Competition dives

There are two main types of diving competition: *springboard diving*, performed from the one-metre and three-metre springboards, and *highboard diving*, performed from either the five- or the ten-metre boards, both of which are firm platforms.

Competitive diving has four main groups of dives: forward dives, back dives, reverse dives and inward dives. There are also dives done with a twist, and there are dives done from a handstand position (from the highboard only) which has to be held steady right on the edge of the board. By and large, the degree of difficulty of a dive increases with the number of twists and somersaults to be performed before entry.

Forward dive: rotating forwards from a forward take-off, that is, with the diver facing the pool.

Back dive: rotating backwards from a back take-off, that is, with the diver facing the board and with his back to the pool.

Reverse dives: rotating backwards from a forward take-off.

Inward dives: rotating forwards from a back take-off.

SCORING IN A DIVING COMPETITION

It would clearly be impossible for the judges of a diving competition to assess the difference between easy and difficult dives as well as marking for the divers' actual execution of them. Each dive is therefore given a special 'tariff value' assessed according to its degree of difficulty, and after the judges have indicated their mark for a competitor's performance of a particular dive, the final score is then multiplied by the tariff value.

It would of course be much simpler if every diver performed exactly the same set of dives but with so many variations to inspire good-class divers, this would be impossibly limiting. In each competition therefore there is a *compulsory* section of basic dives which all the competitors must perform, and a *voluntary* section in which they can show off their individual talents in more complicated dives if they wish.

WHAT THE JUDGES ARE LOOKING FOR

Before the start of a diving competition each competitor must present to the officials a complete list of all the dives he intends to perform, and the order in which he will perform them. This must give exact details of each dive (the direction of take-off and position and so on) and cannot be changed after the closing date for entries.

Each judge marks every dive out of a possible maximum of ten points, with half points awarded if necessary. When five or more judges are used (and this is the case in most national and international competitions) the highest and the lowest marks awarded for each dive are discounted. The remaining marks are then averaged to arrive at the final mark. This system helps to make the result fairer by eliminating any undue bias, either favourable or unfavourable.

Whenever possible judges should be stationed on both sides of the diving board to give a good view of the line of the dive and the entry. Once he has taken up his position no judge should change his place during the event. It is important that he should assess *all* the competitors from the same viewpoint.

The referee will announce the diver, indicate the dive to be performed, and will then blow a whistle or give some other signal for the diver to begin.

The judges must check that the actual dive intended has in fact been performed according to the rules and according to the description given for it. Marks will be deducted if the diver departs either from the rules or from his description. The dive will be judged *as a whole and complete movement,* and although the various phases (the run, take-off, flight and entry) will be considered and will – obviously – affect the final mark, they will not be marked separately and then added together.

Survival swimming

Swimming for fun, for the excitement of a race, or just for the sheer exhilarating pleasure of it – that, happily is all that most swimmers are ever called on to do. Yet every year a large number of individuals are faced with the most powerful of all reasons for learning to swim: personal survival following some sort of water accident. In such situations a strong, competent swimmer who has mastered the skills explained in this book stands the best chance. But even a non-swimmer can help to save his own life if he has a knowledge of additional special survival techniques to use in emergency situations.

The next six pages of this book are devoted to describing some of these special skills. They should be practised to a high degree of proficiency. But remember always that the key to personal survival and life saving is the all-important combination of correct swimming techniques and the endurance to keep it up for a long period or over a considerable distance.

Statistics show that a lot of people panic in emergency situations and create unnecessary problems for themselves, making their situation worse instead of better. For example, even people who can swim fairly well may become alarmed and very ill at ease on finding themselves at risk in the water. They may be quite unaware that the human body is naturally buoyant and that as long as there is air in the lungs it will remain at the surface of the water. This fact is the basis for a most important survival skill: *drownproofing.*

DROWNPROOFING

Drownproofing is really an extension of a normal float and an extremely efficient way of staying on the surface and conserving your energy if you have to face the prospect of a long wait before help arrives. The swimmer's main concern is to stay completely

Above: side-stroke makes breathing easy and is a very useful stroke to use in choppy water.

Right: Treading water is another simple but valuable survival skill. If you keep up a pressure on the water by pressing down with your hands and making a treading movement with your feet, you can keep your head above the surface without using much energy.

Left: Using inflated trousers for flotation.

Below: the air in your lungs will give you a natural buoyancy that will keep you afloat without effort if you learn the technique of 'drownproofing' described on this page.

relaxed and at ease, relying on natural buoyancy to stay afloat. Try it for yourself: lie with your face in the water, arms out to the sides and breath comfortably held. Maintain this position until you need to take another breath, and then give a slight downward kick, at the same time pushing down with your hands and lifting your mouth clear. The breath can be taken either to the front or – in rough water, for example – by turning your head to one side and breathing in the trough created by your head. Once the breath is in you can return to your original relaxed position again, floating face down.

The lower part of your body and your legs will tend to sink down in the water to a more or less natural position, depending on your individual buoyancy. You should allow this to happen, confident in the knowledge that the air in your lungs will keep you up at the surface indefinitely.

If you practise this skill, the possibility of remaining in the water for a long period will hold no fears for you.

TREADING WATER

Drownproofing is a useful technique in situations where it is necessary to stay near a particular spot for any length of time until help arrives. But when a swimmer in difficulties needs to look around for help or signal for it, he must remain vertical in the water, head held well clear of the surface. One way of doing this is by *treading water.*

This is a simple skill that again enables the swimmer to stay in one spot. It is a treading motion, with both feet and hands used to press down on the water in order to push the head above the surface. The swimmer executes a breast-stroke type kick and combines it with a continuous sculling motion of the hands, palms facing downwards and pushing from side to side in small movements.

Begin by practising this skill in water that reaches to just below your mouth when you stand on the pool bottom. Gradually increase the length of time you tread water, and then introduce variations such as using legs only, or arms only, or one leg and one arm, and so on.

SURFACE DIVING

This skill is useful if you have to swim under any barriers, dangerous surface debris, or even burning oil on the surface. It is also the best way of going down to collect an object from the bottom.

FEET-FIRST SURFACE DIVE

From an upright position in the water kick down hard. This will lift the upper part of your body clear of the surface. Now stretch your arms sharply above your head with a strong upward movement and bring your feet and legs together with toes pointed. Your body will now sink very quickly towards the bottom, driven there by the weight that was pushed above the surface. When you reach the desired depth simply arch your back and let your feet slide out backwards or curl up, ready to swim forwards.

HEAD-FIRST SURFACE DIVE

Again the weight of part of the body pushed out of the water is used to drive the whole of the swimmer

Feet-first surface dive: kick down hard on the water and stretch your arms above your head as your body is pushed above the surface. With feet and legs together, let your body sink down again. When you reach the desired depth, arch your back and let your feet slide out behind you. You will then be in a position to swim forwards.

Head-first surface dive: start by swimming breast stroke. Breathe deeply, push your hands downwards and duck your head below the surface. Jack-knife at the hips so that your legs and feet are pushed above the surface. Stretch into as vertical a position as you can and let your own body weight carry you down into the water. You can stop the dive at any depth you choose by turning your head and hands towards the surface.

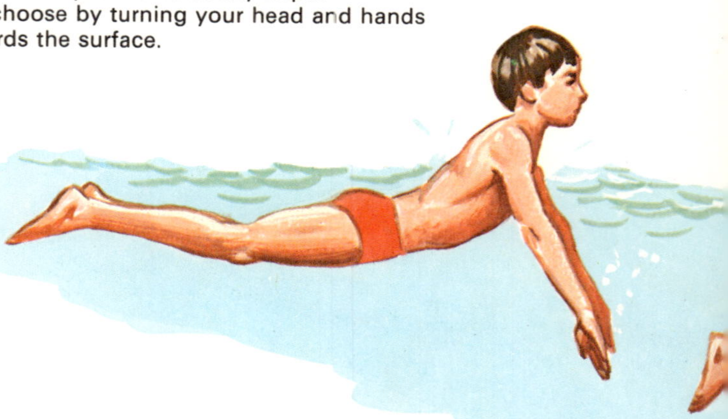

downwards. This time it is the *legs* that are pushed above the surface.

Start by swimming breast stroke, take a deep breath and bob your head sharply below the surface, stretching your hands towards the bottom. Now jack-knife at the hips and your feet and legs will be lifted out of the water. Push them upwards and stretch your body into a streamlined position, as vertical as possible. You will then be carried down in a dive which you can stop at any moment you choose by turning your hands and head back towards the surface, more or less as shown in the illustration on page 44.

HOW TO USE CLOTHES AS FLOATS

Learning to use various articles of clothing to assist in flotation is a source of great fun as well as being a very practical skill in times of emergency. The tricky part of the manoeuvre is in removing the clothes in the water, especially any that have to be pulled over the head. A few sessions practising in the pool with a pair of pyjamas will soon make you skilful, though shirts and blouses with long sleeves, trousers and skirts are the most suitable articles for floats. Once off, the aim is to seal off all the openings except one and then trap air inside the garment and use it as a float. There are many ingenious variations on this theme. Try to devise some of them in the pool.

ENTERING THE WATER FROM A HEIGHT

If you have to jump into the water from a height, it is safer to do so from a one-footed take-off as this helps you to keep a better balance in the air and will prevent you from hitting the water with the wrong part of your body.

If you intend to make a *shallow* entry, spread your legs and arms to cause a resistance to the water. But remember that, when jumping from a height of more than a couple of metres, this method can be dangerous and unpleasant, so a *compact body position* should be held until your body actually enters the water.

DISTANCE SWIMMING

This is the most important of all the survival skills and should be practised regularly. The ability to keep going steadily without stopping is more important than speed or style, although obviously a well-executed stroke will be more efficient and will take less of the available energy.

Whether you use the crawl, breast stroke or side-stroke, a long, slow stroke should be used for distance swimming.

Side-stroke (a variation of the breast stroke) is a very valuable technique in survival and life-saving situations, the main advantage being that, with his face resting on the surface, the swimmer can breathe behind the bow wave. He combines a simplified scissors-type kick with what is basically a breast-stroke arm action done on the side. The lower arm stretches out ahead of the swimmer, making a much smaller circle than the other arm, which starts its circling action in front of the face and continues its pull almost right down to the thigh.

Many a swimmer has got himself out of trouble with the techniques described on this page. Start practising now.

Chin carry: this is an easy way to tow someone who is relaxed or unconscious.

Life-saving

As in personal survival, being a good strong swimmer is your most important asset if you have to go to the rescue of anyone in difficulty in the water. But strength and the ability to perform all the other useful life-saving skills will be useless unless you also know the best procedures to follow in certain emergency situations before you are actually faced with them. This means that you must be aware of the commonest hazards in water rescue situations, and know the rules and principles of water safety, which are fully explained in the various manuals issued by life-saving and accident prevention societies all over the world.

This chapter deals with some of the main points in life saving and demonstrates skills which you should practise to a high degree of efficiency with a friend *in the safe environment of the swimming pool.*

REAL-LIFE RESCUES

In a real life situation if you spot someone in distress in the water the first thing to do is to draw the attention of anyone else near at hand and assess the situation for the correct course of action. Is it a situation that you can tackle successfully alone? Or is it one in which additional help is needed? And what is the best means of rescue? Obviously the decision will depend on the particular situation with which you are faced in relation to your own swimming strength and ability, but *speed* is the vital ingredient of *all* attempted rescues.

Your own safety must be considered too: no purpose is served by a poor swimmer plunging into rough water. The result would be *two* swimmers in trouble instead of one. The victim needs help not company. You must therefore decide immediately what is the safest and most practical method of rescue *that is likely to succeed.* And always assure the victim that help is at hand.

It is not always necessary to *swim* to the victim's aid. In fact, the recognised order of preference for making a single-handed rescue attempt is: *reach, throw, wade, row, swim* and *tow.*

Reach. If the victim is close enough to grasp an outstretched hand or can be reached with a pole, a length of rope or a piece of clothing, then this is the best method of rescue, so long as the rescuer anchors himself securely to some fixed object on the bank or shore or takes up a very firm position. A swimmer in difficulties is likely to pull hard, and possibly frantically at anything within his reach, and his struggles could drag the rescuer in after him.

Throw. A lifebelt with a rope attached is the ideal thing to throw to the victim. But again the rescuer must make sure that he is securely anchored to some onshore object or firmly braced against it. If no lifebelt is to hand there are often other objects which will at least help to keep the victim up at the surface until further help arrives – spars of wood or a largish tree branch – anything in fact that is buoyant. Take care not to hit the victim as you throw.

Wade. If the victim is in or near shallow water the rescuer will wade to his help if the bottom is sound, still taking care that his own position is secure before

Chest tow: this gives the rescuer a firm grip on the victim.

reaching out to the victim.

Row. A nearby boat makes the perfect rescue apparatus. But check first that it is seaworthy, and watch that the victim does not capsize it as he is taken aboard.

Swim. A rescuer who decides that the best method is to swim should take with him some form of support for the victim – a lifebelt or a piece of wood. Every effort should be made to avoid direct physical contact with the victim lest in sheer panic he struggles and overcomes or tires his rescuer.

Tow. You should attempt a tow rescue *only if you are a very strong swimmer indeed and experienced in this kind of rescue,* or if the victim is so exhausted that he is quite passive.

LIFE-SAVING PRACTICES IN THE POOL

The towing techniques described here can be practised *in a swimming pool* with a friend, and it is every swimmer's duty to be able to perform them reasonably well. But being able to tow a willing and far-from-exhausted body in the quiet calm of a swimming pool is no guarantee that you will be able to do so, still half-clad perhaps, with a struggling victim in a stretch of cold open river or lake water. Strong currents and winds are other hazards not encountered in mock rescues in the pool. Nevertheless as long as these differences between the mock rescue and a real emergency are kept in mind your ability to tow well may make the difference between a life lost and a life saved.

Approaching the victim. A rescuer must be able to see where he is going and what is happening to the victim. Breast stroke, therefore, is the best to use for your approach, with feet and legs held ready to push away from the victim if he makes a panicky grab at you. (The various ways of releasing yourself from a grab are described in most life-saving manuals).

Building up towing stamina. Practise the tows with a partner over a short distance at first. Start with the width or even half the width of the pool. Once you can cope with this distance, increase it to a length and go on building up from there. Always try to maintain good stroke style because this means *efficient* strokes. And make sure that the victim's face and mouth are kept above the waterline.

If you have difficulty towing your mock victim at first, try increasing his buoyancy by giving him a couple of floats or an inflatable ring to hold on to. When your technique has improved, he can discard them again.

Try competing with several other pairs of swimmers to see who can perform the fastest rescue from the poolside, remembering that a real-life victim may have stopped breathing and be in immediate need of artificial respiration, and speed is therefore vital.

Artificial respiration. This is another essential skill which everyone, swimmers and non-swimmers alike, should be able to perform. Details of the actual techniques are fully explained in life-saving and first aid manuals. Their practice is an important part of the preparation for real-life rescues.

Once you can swim

Once you can swim reasonably well, the best way of improving still further is to join a local swimming club. Clubs are well organised and cater for groups of all ages and all levels of swimming ability. If you have talent for swimming or diving, a club offers every opportunity for testing it in time trials and competitive races. If you swim well enough, you may be chosen to represent the club in local or regional competitions, and eventually the door may open to national and even international events.

But even if you are not all that keen on the competitive aspect of swimming, your performance will improve in the company of other (and possibly better) swimmers. And there are many associated club activities of interest. Boys may find excitement and challenge in water polo, and girls may become enthusiasts of synchronised swimming, an increasingly popular form of swimming in which the swimmers perform graceful ballet-type movements and formations to the accompaniment of music. These related sports are great fun in themselves, as well as providing opportunities for meeting people who share your interests.

Most clubs provide coaching in both swimming and diving and give their members a chance to work for some of the many personal proficiency and incentive awards made by local and national organisations (the bronze, silver and gold life saving awards of the Royal Life Saving Society, for example). The tests for the various awards are interesting and progressive, with certificates and sew-on badges awarded to prove the prowess of swimmers who reach the required standard for each grade.

WELCOME TO THE WATER WORLD

The basic skills described in this book are aimed at improving your all-round swimming ability but once you can swim and dive efficiently and are able to swim safely in open water, they are only the first introduction to a whole range of fascinating water sports. But because there is an element of risk in *any* water activity, even for the strongest swimmer, use common sense before venturing into or on to water, whatever your purpose.

Never swim or sail in unfamiliar water without first checking with local lifeguards that the spot you have chosen is safe and suitable for your particular activity. Many safe-looking and attractive places become dangerous when the tide or current changes, or if an offshore wind springs up unexpectedly.

Always check on what lies beneath the surface of any open stretch of water. This is a fairly obvious thing to do if you plan to dive, but even if you are going to swim, or just walk round a headland, it is better to take stock first. Mud, rocks, reeds, a sharply shelving shoreline – all these can be hazards. Old jetties and piers – often a source of interest and fun – can also be dangerous because they often produce whirlpool effects immediately below them, setting a hidden trap for the unwary or the foolhardy swimmer who ventures too close.

Never swim alone. And *never* stay in the water too

long as cramp attacks cold muscles very easily.

Never swim too far out; your fatigued muscles will have to cope with the same distance back again.

Always swim parallel to the shore line of lake or sea, never away from it.

Never swim beyond your depth in open water.

Never follow a beach ball or inflatable airbed out into open water. If they should get carried off by wind or tide, *let them go.*

Always keep well clear of any area that is marked off for water skiiers or power boats. And *always* observe warning notices restricting swimming or drawing attention to any hazard whatever.

If you are canoeing, sailing or just playing about in a boat, *wear a life-jacket,* even though you may consider yourself a good strong swimmer. A bump on the head can easily daze you or knock you out. A good life-jacket will keep you safe and in the right position until you recover or until help arrives.

If you do capsize a canoe or small boat, don't swim away from your craft. The best plan is to stay with it. Hold on to it and allow the air trapped underneath or inside to keep you afloat and safe. Hold on to one end and if you are near enough and the craft is light enough, kick your way to the nearest landing point.

If you make a point of following these common-sense water rules you will enjoy your water sports in safety – and without endangering the life of anyone who has to come to your rescue.

AGE GROUP SWIMMING

Interest in competitive swimming has increased enormously at all levels in recent years but one of the most exciting things is the growth of 'age group swimming'. Beginning in the United States in the 1950s, this has now spread to almost every country in the world. Organised by the national body governing swimming in each country, competitions are arranged between young swimmers of the same age range. The events are usually arranged in two-year steps: for example, 12 and 13-year-olds will compete against each other in the same races. The racing distances vary according to the age group but in some places, particularly in Australia, even the youngest competitors are given the chance to race over fairly long distances (up to 1500 metres).

Most swimming clubs now have Age Group teams, and arrange special training and practice sessions for them.

Because swimming performances can be measured so easily against a stopwatch, it is now possible to compare standards anywhere in the world, and gradually more international meetings and tours are being organised for young swimmers who have reached the same standards in different countries. So the chance of travelling locally, nationally and abroad to compete is now open to any young swimmer who is keen and enthusiastic enough to practise and train. You could be one of them!

Even if you don't specialise in synchronised swimming, you and your friends can have fun making this 'washing tub' formation and other simple patterns of movement.